AF751080

Intellectual Property

Edited by Sakthivel Lakshmana Prabu
and Timmakkondu Narasimman
Kuppusami Suriyaprakash

Published in London, United Kingdom

IntechOpen

Supporting open minds since 2005

Intellectual Property
http://dx.doi.org/10.5772/intechopen.94621
Edited by Sakthivel Lakshmana Prabu and Timmakkondu Narasimman Kuppusami Suriyaprakash

Contributors
Francis Kariuki, Ojeswini Bondalapati, Bency Baby T, Timmakkondu Narasimman Kuppusami Suriyaprakash, Fabio Monteiro Dos Santos, Ricardo Carvalho Rodrigues, Heleno José Costa Bezerra Netto, Cesar Vianna Moreira Jr, Daniel Golodne, Sakthivel Lakshmana Prabu

© The Editor(s) and the Author(s) 2022
The rights of the editor(s) and the author(s) have been asserted in accordance with the Copyright, Designs and Patents Act 1988. All rights to the book as a whole are reserved by INTECHOPEN LIMITED. The book as a whole (compilation) cannot be reproduced, distributed or used for commercial or non-commercial purposes without INTECHOPEN LIMITED's written permission. Enquiries concerning the use of the book should be directed to INTECHOPEN LIMITED rights and permissions department (permissions@intechopen.com).
Violations are liable to prosecution under the governing Copyright Law.

Individual chapters of this publication are distributed under the terms of the Creative Commons Attribution 3.0 Unported License which permits commercial use, distribution and reproduction of the individual chapters, provided the original author(s) and source publication are appropriately acknowledged. If so indicated, certain images may not be included under the Creative Commons license. In such cases users will need to obtain permission from the license holder to reproduce the material. More details and guidelines concerning content reuse and adaptation can be found at http://www.intechopen.com/copyright-policy.html.

Notice
Statements and opinions expressed in the chapters are these of the individual contributors and not necessarily those of the editors or publisher. No responsibility is accepted for the accuracy of information contained in the published chapters. The publisher assumes no responsibility for any damage or injury to persons or property arising out of the use of any materials, instructions, methods or ideas contained in the book.

First published in London, United Kingdom, 2022 by IntechOpen
IntechOpen is the global imprint of INTECHOPEN LIMITED, registered in England and Wales, registration number: 11086078, 5 Princes Gate Court, London, SW7 2QJ, United Kingdom
Printed in Croatia

British Library Cataloguing-in-Publication Data
A catalogue record for this book is available from the British Library

Additional hard and PDF copies can be obtained from orders@intechopen.com

Intellectual Property
Edited by Sakthivel Lakshmana Prabu and Timmakkondu Narasimman Kuppusami Suriyaprakash
p. cm.
Print ISBN 978-1-83968-920-8
Online ISBN 978-1-83968-921-5
eBook (PDF) ISBN 978-1-83968-922-2

For EU product safety concerns:
IN TECH d.o.o., Prolaz Marije Krucifikse Kozulić 3, 51000 Rijeka, Croatia, info@intechopen.com or visit our website at intechopen.com.

We are IntechOpen, the world's leading publisher of Open Access books

Built by scientists, for scientists

5,700+
Open access books available

140,000+
International authors and editors

175M+
Downloads

156
Countries delivered to

Our authors are among the
Top 1%
most cited scientists

12.2%
Contributors from top 500 universities

CLARIVATE ANALYTICS BOOK CITATION INDEX INDEXED

WEB OF SCIENCE™

Selection of our books indexed in the Book Citation Index (BKCI)
in Web of Science Core Collection™

Interested in publishing with us?
Contact book.department@intechopen.com

Numbers displayed above are based on latest data collected.
For more information visit www.intechopen.com

Meet the editors

Dr. Sakthivel Lakshman Prabu obtained a Ph.D. from Manipal University, India. He pursued a post-graduate diploma in Intellectual Property Law from the National Law School of India University, Bangalore. He has been working at Anna University, Birla Institute of Technology and Science, Tiruchirappalli, India since 2009. Dr. Prabu has more than 20 years of experience both in reputed pharmaceutical industries and academic institutions. He has published more than 100 peer-reviewed publications in international and national journals, authored 22 book chapters, and edited 6 books. He also has four patents to his credit. Dr. Prabu serves as a reviewer and editorial board member for various journals and he has organized various national and international conferences, trainings, workshops, and symposiums. He has received funding for several projects from various government funding agencies in India.

Dr. TNK Suriyaprakash is a proud alumnus of Madurai Medical College, India, and Birla Institute of Technology and Science, Pilani, India. He obtained a Ph.D. in Pharmaceutical Technology from the Tamil Nadu Dr. MGR Medical University, Chennai, India. Dr. Suriyaprakash has published more than fifty original research and review papers in reputed journals, authored two books and thirteen book chapters, as well as edited three books. Two of his research works have been published by Indian Patent Office, Chennai. To date, he has received the equivalent of $50,000 USD in research grants from various funding agencies. During his tenure as principal there, the Al Shifa College of Pharmacy, Kerala, India has been recognized as a top-ranked college for the past five years by the Ministry of Human Resource Department (MHRD), New Delhi, and as one of the best colleges by the Institution Innovative Council, MHRD.

Contents

Preface

The development and status of a country is based on the country's intellectual property. The number of patent applications has never been greater and there are several examples that patents have helped support the development of an ever-increasing range of technology. However, this success has not given rise to universal satisfaction, either within the immediate circle of administrators and users of the patent system or among the intended beneficiaries of the system more widely in society. Worldwide, the system today faces two big challenges: an internal challenge concerning the actual operation of the system, and an external challenge concerning the policy role and the economic and social impact of the patent system.

This book, *Intellectual Property*, discusses issues pertaining to intellectual property rights, specifically patents and patent-related issues. It considers divergent issues related to patents starting from invention to filing of a patent and the issues that come along with it. The contributing authors come from various countries and backgrounds, thus providing a global perspective of the subject.

The editors of this volume, Sakthivel Lakshmana Prabu and TNK Suriyaprakash, have more than three decades of experience in the pharmaceutical industry, academia, and regulations. They also have several patents to their credit.

The book begins with an introductory chapter, "Introductory Chapter: Acquisition of Intellectual Property Rights in International Markets - Where Do We Start?" by Sakthivel Lakshmana Prabu and Timmakkondu Narasimman Kuppusami Suriyaprakash, which discusses the genesis of patenting and patent-related issues and analyzes the global scenario at length.

Chapter 2, "Patents - Understanding the Facts" by Ojeswini Bondalapati, discusses the nuances of writing a patent application and defending it through examination.

Chapter 3, "Intellectual Property Rights: Bioprospecting, Biopiracy and Protection of Traditional Knowledge - An Indian Perspective" by Bency Baby T and TNK Suriyaprakash, provides information relevant to national and legal rules and policies regarding intellectual property rights. Protection of traditional knowledge and conservation of the rights of local and indigenous peoples to their knowledge and resources are equally important. In this regard, the chapter also discusses the concepts of biopiracy and bioprospecting.

Chapter 4, "Harnessing Traditional Knowledge Holders' Institutions in Realising Sustainable Development Goals in Kenya" by Francis Kariuki, examines the role of traditional knowledge (TK) holders' institutions in the realization of components of Sustainable Development Goals (SDGs) 9 and 16.

Chapter 5, "A Methodology for Evaluation and Distribution of Patent Applications to INPI-BR Patent Examiners: A Case Study in the Electricity Field" by Cesar Vianna Moreira Júnior, Daniel Marques Golodne, and Ricardo Carvalho Rodrigues, discusses the development of a new methodology for evaluation and distribution of patent applications in the field of electricity to the examiners at the Brazilian Patent Office (INPI). It examines the classification of these applications according to the International Patent Classification (IPC) along with the variables corresponding to the volume of data of the application and its complexity for the examination process.

Chapter 6, "Comparative Analysis of Appeal Procedures in the European, American and Brazilian Patent Offices" by Fabio Monteiro dos Santos, Heleno José Costa Bezerra Netto, and Ricardo Carvalho Rodrigues, compares the laws, regulations, rules, and procedures of appeals in the European Patent Office (EPO), the United States Patent and Trademark Office (USPTO), and the Brazilian Patent Office (INPI), pointing out the main differences between them.

This book is a useful resource for research scholars, students, industrial experts, technologists.

We acknowledge full support of all the contributing authors as well as the staff at IntechOpen for their help in completing this book.

Sakthivel Lakshmana Prabu
Department of Pharmaceutical Technology,
University College of Engineering (BIT Campus),
Anna University,
Tiruchirappalli, Tamil Nadu, India

Timmakkondu Narasimman Kuppusami Suriyaprakash
Professor,
Department of Pharmaceutics,
Al Shifa College of Pharmacy,
Perinthalmanna, Kerala, India

Section 1

Overview of IPR and Patents

Chapter 1

Introductory Chapter: Acquisition of Intellectual Property Rights in International Markets - Where Do We Start?

Sakthivel Lakshmana Prabu
and Timmakkondu Narasimman Kuppusami Suriyaprakash

1. Introduction

1.1 What is property?

Property is simply a collection of rights arising from the concepts of ownership and possession in the legal sense. While most of them have a physical existence, the importance or significance of property is determined by the knowledge of its intended purpose.

Only when there is an idea/technology, it has been utilized as a matter in such a way that it can meet a human need/demand does it become resource. Either idea or technology becomes a resource in two ways, and they are

1. Material resource

2. Intellectual or technological resource.

Altogether the property rights are restricted or constrained by other people's rights. Each property right is outlined and established in practice to ensure that it is balanced with other property rights.

1.2 What is intellectual property?

Intellectual property is a type of property generated/created by the human minds based on their intelligence. Novelty or originality of this intellectual property diverges from one system to the others, which has a finite life span [1].

According to intellectual property, ideas are a representation of the creator's identity or self, which need to be protected.

1.2.1 Intellectual property rights

Different rights such as Patents, trademarks, copyrights, protection of undisclosed information, traditional knowledge, geographical indicators, industrial designs, and integrated circuits as layout designs are examples of intellectual property rights, which are recognized by the Trade Related Intellectual Property

IntechOpen

Rights Agreement (TRIPS) and governed by the World Trade Organization (WTO) (World Trading Organization).

Intellectual property rights are the rights granted to individuals over their mental inventions, and they grant an exclusive right to the inventor to utilize their product for a set length of time. This exclusive right to the inventor for their invention can encourage the technical process by

1. Inspire the innovation and research.

2. Inspire an innovator to reveal their inventions.

3. Offering award as a prize to help with the costs for creating new inventions.

4. Provides a financial incentive to invest in new lines of production that may or may not be lucrative [2].

1.2.2 International intellectual property regime

Various Congresses in Vienna and the rest of Europe laid the groundwork for International Intellectual Property Protection in the nineteenth century. In 1883, the Paris Convention established the protection of industrial property. In this Paris Convention patents, trademarks and industrial design properties were accorded protection.

The Paris Convention established the first international trademark legislation and the concept of a well-known mark. For countries that are members of the Paris Convention, special unions and arrangements have been formed. Also in this Paris Convention, fundamental principles of Madrid agreement were outlined and represented. This Madrid Agreement is a unique agreement that was established to standardize trademarks [3–5].

Protection of literary and artistic works was framed in Berne Convention during 1886, and subsequently, International Copyright Act was passed [6].

The General Agreement on Tariffs and Trade (GATT) was negotiated on Trade and Employment Conference held in the United Nations even after negotiating governments failed to establish the International Trade Organization (ITO). The GATT was established in 1949 and lasted until 1993, when it was succeeded by the World Trade Organization, which was established in 1995 [7, 8].

The World Intellectual Property Organization (WIPO) was created in 1960, which governs both the Paris and Berne Conventions. These conventions led to establish the World Intellectual Property Organization (WIPO) in 1967 [9].

The United Nations Conference on Trade and Development (UNCTAD) was founded in 1964 to provide a venue to discuss issues concerning their economic development for developing countries. The organization's goals are to help developing countries to maximize their trade, investment, and development prospects. In addition, the organization assists the developing countries for their efforts to integrate into the global economy fairly [10].

In 1960, global trade expanded substantially, and various National Governments realized the necessity of setting norms and rules worldwide to integrate the disparate National and regional regulations that had previously controlled. In 1966, the United Nations General Assembly established the United Nations Commission on International Trade Law (UNCITRAL) to promote the progressive harmonization and unification of international trade law [11].

World Trade Organization (WTO) was established in the year 1995 and it has become an international organization for understanding the various IPR [12].

Several corporate organizations to ensure their continued growth, higher profits, and leadership in market premeditated their project management system for

- Utilization of the inter-/intra-knowledge base to its full potential.
- Management of IPR on a strategic level.
- Receiving knowledge and inventions as inputs from various external sources.
- Managing the collaborative research by internal expertise members.
- Provide mutually beneficial licenses among the knowledge ownerships.

In the future, the developing prospect will look for effective linkages between increasing societal rivalry on the one hand and establishing legal ownership of innovations on the other hand.

Knowledge, technology management, and process are incorporated in the intertwined societal, moral, and ethical challenges as the influencing approached for the several international trade.

2. Resolution of new dimension and disputes

In the upcoming decades, this technology explores new dimensions from unknown paths. This IPR will encourage for more innovation and knowledge sharing between this highly competitive networks. Various intertwined IPR are

- Domain names and trademarks: In cyberspace, copyright is protected.
- Traditional knowledge, prior art, material transfer agreements, and bio-prospecting rights are all protected.
- Patents and software.
- Biotechnological inventions.
- Optional compulsory licensing, border measures, parallel imports, and IPR exhaustion
- Export of technology is regulated by the government [13].

3. Significance of IPR in developing countries

During that time, an extensive debate has been taken place about the restrictions of Intellectual Property Rights on the developing countries.

The relative intensity of their technical activity determines the potential significance of IPR in developing countries. Developing countries agreed to the TRIPS agreement for various reasons, ranging from the prospect of increased access to rich countries' agricultural and clothing markets to the belief that stronger intellectual property rights would foster more knowledge transfer and innovation. However, in many countries, particularly in the poorest, the long-term advantages are unknown and costly to attain. But they believe that they will be having a favorable impact by enforcing the IPR. It also points out that IPRs have had variable degrees of growth effects at different eras and in different parts of the world, with countries achieving high growth rates under varying degrees of IPR protection. Stronger IPRs undoubtedly have short-term consequences for poor countries, such as higher pricing for technology and protected items [14].

3.1 Impression of stronger IPR in developing countries

Benefits of exclusive rights to innovations are

a. Inspiration of innovations by private organization and other enterprises.

b. For productive activity utilizing the new knowledge.

c. Spreading the new knowledge to the other organization [15].

4. Intellectual property rights

Intellectual property rights are broadly divided into two main areas.
They are copyright and related rights and industrial property.

4.1 Copyright and related rights

Copyright protects the rights of writers of literary and artistic works, which includes books, writings, paintings, musical compositions, sculpture, films, and computer programs for a minimum of 50 years after the author's death after the work is published.

The rights of performers like actors, musicians, and singers; creators of phonograms such as sound recordings; and broadcasting companies are also protected by copyright and related rights, which is referred as neighboring rights.

The main purpose of copyright and related rights protection is to stimulate and reward the innovative creative work.

5. Industrial property

Industrial property is broadly divided into two main areas.

One area is the protection of distinctive signs, such as trademarks (which differentiate the goods, products, or services from those of others) and geographical indications (which identify a product as coming from a location where a specific characteristic of the product is essentially attributable to its geographical origin). The primary goal of trademark protection is to encourage and ensure fair competition, as well as to safeguard customers by allowing them to make educated decisions about diverse goods and services. If the symbol in question remains distinctive, the protection may extend eternally.

Other sorts of industrial property are safeguarded largely to encourage inspire innovation, design, and creation of technology development. Patented inventions, industrial designs, and trade secrets are all included in this category.

The social goal is to protect the results of investments in new technology development, thereby providing an incentive and means to fund research and development operations. Foreign direct investment, joint ventures, and licensing should all be made easier by a functioning intellectual property law. Typically, protection is granted for a set period of time (typically 20 years in the case of patents).

Intellectual property protection laws are founded on a variety of philosophical underpinnings and philosophies. In the area of tangible property, the majority of these notions are rotten. Intellectual property is fundamentally distinct from other types of property in some ways. Philosophical arguments are frequently employed to outline and define the bounds and breadth of protection in an age when intellectual regimes are being strengthened, reinterpreted, and challenged. As a result, it is critical to investigate and comprehend these arguments.

6. Conclusion

This IPR can protect the ideas and inspire the innovations, stimulating the creation of technology and innovations and design. Different types of IPR are designed, which can provide benefits by sharing the new invention as knowledge and assisting the technology transfer through licensing. Also, inspire the invention with joint venture for further development. The potential significance of IPR in developing countries is protecting their investment as incentives and inspire further development in the research, which can help to attain the desired technology advancement and economical status in this global competitive. IPR is the only key element in attaining the social, economic, and technological advancement.

Author details

Sakthivel Lakshmana Prabu[1]*
and Timmakkondu Narasimman Kuppusami Suriyaprakash[2]

1 Department of Pharmaceutical Technology, University College of Engineering (BIT Campus), Anna University, Tiruchirappalli, Tamil Nadu, India

2 Department of Pharmaceutics, Al Shifa College of Pharmacy, Poonthavanam, Kerala, India

*Address all correspondence to: slaxmanvel@gmail.com

IntechOpen

© 2021 The Author(s). Licensee IntechOpen. This chapter is distributed under the terms of the Creative Commons Attribution License (http://creativecommons.org/licenses/by/3.0), which permits unrestricted use, distribution, and reproduction in any medium, provided the original work is properly cited.

References

[1] Ramakrishna T. Basic Principles & Acquisition of Intellectual Property Rights. Bangalore, India: CIPRA, NLSIU, 2005. pp. 1-11

[2] What is Intellectual Property Rights. WIPO, Geneva, Switzerland: WIPO; 2020. Available from: https://www.wipo.int/about-ip/en/

[3] Summary of this Paris Convention for the protection of Industrial Property. WIPO, Geneva, Switzerland: WIPO; 1883. Available from: https://www.wipo.int/treaties/en/ip/paris/summary_paris.html

[4] WIPO National Seminar on Intellectual Property. WIPO/IP/CAI/1/03/2. WIPO, Geneva, Switzerland: WIPO; 2003. Available from: https://www.wipo.int/edocs/mdocs/arab/en/2003/ip_cai_1/pdf/wipo_ip_cai_1_03_2.pdf

[5] Summary of the Madrid Agreement Concerning the International Registration of Marks (1891) and the Protocol Relating to that Agreement. WIPO, Geneva, Switzerland: WIPO; 1989. Available from: https://www.wipo.int/treaties/en/registration/madrid/summary_madrid_marks.html

[6] Summary of the Berne Convention for the Protection of Literary and Artistic Works. WIPO, Geneva, Switzerland: WIPO; 1886. Available from: https://www.wipo.int/treaties/en/ip/berne/summary_berne.html

[7] The WTO Agreement Series-General Agreement on Tariffs and Trade. Genève, Switzerland: WTO; 1998. Available from: https://www.wto.org/english/res_e/booksp_e/agrmntseries2_gatt_e.pdf

[8] Available from: http://en.wikipedia.org/wiki/General_Agreement_on_Tariffs_and_Trade

[9] Summary of the Convention Establishing the World Intellectual Property Organization. WIPO, Geneva, Switzerland: WIPO Convention; 1967. Available from: https://www.wipo.int/treaties/en/convention/summary_wipo_convention.html

[10] United Nations Conference on Trade and Development. WIKIPEDIA; Available from: https://en.wikipedia.org/wiki/United_Nations_Conference_on_Trade_and_Development

[11] United Nations Commission on International Trade Law. WIKIPEDIA; Available from: http://en.wikipedia.org/wiki/United_Nations_Commission_on_International_Trade_Law

[12] WTO in Brief. Genève, Switzerland: WTO; Available from: https://www.wto.org/english/thewto_e/whatis_e/inbrief_e/inbr_e.htm

[13] Ganguli P. Patents and patent information in 1979 and 2004: A perspective from India. World Patent Information. 2004;**26**:61-62

[14] Lall S. Indicators of the relative importance of IPRs in developing countries. Research Policy. 2003;**32**:1657

[15] Hassan E, Yaqub O, Diepeveen S. Intellectual Property and Developing Countries A review of the Literature. Santa Monica, CA: RAND Corporation; 2010. Available from: https://www.rand.org/content/dam/rand/pubs/technical_reports/2010/RAND_TR804.pdf

Chapter 2

Patents - Understanding the Facts

Ojeswini Bondalapati

Abstract

Patent is a well know term but, there is still uncertainty existing about the Patent system. Patents is a form of intellectual property (IP) that represent an invention, or it can be considered as one of the intangible assets which grants an exclusive right for exploitation of an invention for a limited period of time. There are few misconceptions existing around the patent terminology which is leading to a number of ineffective patents and more precisely, the importance of patents is less known even in academic and industry sectors. Patents are key to innovation which can lead in strategic management of economy. Big corporates are major players in the market who are reaping maximum benefits of the patent's portfolio whereas, small scale entities even though they are striving to drive towards innovation, they are failing to protect their intellectual property in form of patents. Even if they are succeeding in protecting such ideas in form of inventions, still they are unable to benefit to maximum, due to lack of proper management of their IP portfolio.

Keywords: Intellectual Property, innovation, intangible assets, Patents, Patent Law, Novelty, inventive step, IP management, non-patentable, scope of protection, Patent Portfolio

1. Introduction

Intellectual Property defines the intangible assets arisen out of one's intellect. There are different forms of intellectual property like Copyright, Trademarks, Trade Dress, Patents, Trade Secrets, Utility Models, Industrial Designs, Geographical Indications, Traditional Knowledge and Cultural Expressions. Among these assets, Patents involves inventions in form of both product and process. Patent is an exclusive property right granted to the inventor (s) by the respective sovereign body for a limited period.

Patents is still an unresolved subject for most of the educational institutions, startups and small, medium scale sectors. There is an unfilled knowledge gap between these sectors where research and innovation are not inclined towards a proper protection which could increase the value of business to these sectors. Even academic institutions can reap the benefits of research and innovation through reformed IPR policies which is a backdrop in the developing countries. Patents is believed to be costly affair but aftermath of filing of patents, which can pave way to profits and value addition to the business can be devised through IP management strategies. A business entity should be open to innovation that involves IPR management.

It is essential for an inventor and the applicant to know the patent terminology and the Patent Law practiced in respective jurisdiction to acquire effective patents which drive towards innovation. This chapter can state the myths and facts and how to fill existing knowledge gap to attain a sustainable innovation.

2. Understanding patent terminology

There are few patent terminologies to be well understood by an inventor and the applicant of the patent to reap maximum benefits from such inventions. Patent is granted to both product and process.

2.1 Patentability criteria

There are three important criteria to be met by each invention to be qualified as a patent.

2.1.1 Novelty

Novelty defines that the product or process to be new and unknown to public before the filing of the patent application. This criterion prevents the prior art from being patented again. Prior art includes already existing patent applications, granted patents or non-patent literature like journals, research papers, books which disclose the use of technology that is similar to your invention. If your invention is publicly disclosed in technical conferences/seminars or exhibitions, or publicly demonstrated and used before filing the patent, then such invention is not considered as novel. Few countries like U.S.A, India provide a grace period of 12 months from such date of public disclosure to file a patent for such invention.

2.1.2 Inventive step/non-obviousness

The invention shall not be obvious or apparent to a person ordinary skilled in the field relating to the invention (PHOSITA- person having ordinary skill in the art). Basically, the invention shall contain an inventive step over the prior art and such improvement should not be mere improvement or general re-arrangement of components/features of the invention. Illustrations [1] which are considered as obvious are:

- Mere arrangement or rearrangement of known prior art elements according to known methods to yield predictable results.
- Substitution of a known alternative of an element to obtain predictable results.
- Use of known alternative technique to improve similar devices (methods, or products) in the same way.
- Use of known element or method from a finite number of identified, predictable solutions, with a reasonable expectation of success.
- Known method in one field of technology which may prompt variations of it for use in either the same field or a different filed based on design incentives or other market forces, if such variations are predictable to one of ordinary skill in the art.
- Teachings, or suggestions, or motivation in the prior art that would have led one of ordinary skill to modify the prior art reference to arrive at the claimed invention.

2.1.3 Industrial use

Patents in the form of product or process should be able to solve an existing problem or it can be an innovative solution than the existing solutions to a problem and such invention should be used on industrial scale to reach the public.

Myth: Any invention with the above three patentability criteria can be qualified as patent.

Fact: Apart from the above three patentability criteria your invention should not fall under non-inventions criteria.

2.1.4 The non- inventions recognized globally

- Discoveries are non-patentable:

The discovery of laws or principles of nature or science, or any living or non-living material is not patentable subject matter [2].

Reason: since they are already existing in nature and discovering is to uncover something or revelation of existing systems whereas, inventing is to create something unpredictable from available systems.

- Scientific theories are non-patentable:

Scientific theories are non-patentable, regardless of how radical or revolutionary their insights may be since, they are theory. Patents are granted to a product or process which incorporates such theory to bring out innovative solution to an existing problem [2].

- Inventions Contrary to public order or security and morality are non-patentable:

Inventions that cause serious prejudice to human, animal or plant life or health or to the environment are non- patentable since, an invention should be able to solve a problem existing in the public sector but not to create harm to the welfare of public. Examples: a process for cloning human beings; an invention that involves the use of human embryos for industrial or commercial purposes [2].

- Methods for treatment of the human or animal body are non-patentable:

Treatment of humans or animals by surgery, therapy and diagnostic methods are not capable of industrial application, and it is against the policy of practice of medical professionals to restrict other medical practitioners from use of such method of treatment [2].

- Mathematical methods or algorithms are non-patentable:

Mathematical methods are considered a part of theory and solving the problem using such mathematical methods is considered to be a mere mental skill [2].

- Method of playing games is non-patentable:

Playing games is considered as act of mental skill and it can vary from person to person in playing a similar game even when they are pre-defined set of rules since there is always a probability of ways depending on the choice of the player (s) made during each stage of game and such act does not involve technology development and such method or tactics does not have industrial applicability [2].

- Business methods or strategies, or business models are non-patentable:

Business methods or strategies or business models are the methods used for a particular business sector and such methods gain competitive advantage over the competitors in same technology. Such methods or tactics cannot be industrially applicable for every business sector working in same technology [2].

- Presentations of information is non- patentable:

A presentation of information defined solely by the content of the information is not patentable since such representation is non-technical in nature and such works are considered as copyright of such creator [2].

- Esthetic creations are non-patentable:

Esthetic creations relate to an article (e.g., a painting or sculpture) having aspects of art and such works are not technical in nature. Such works do not qualify inventive step I and industrial application rather, the appreciation of such works is essentially subjective in nature.

- Traditional knowledge is non- patentable:

This type of knowledge is passed through generation and it belongs to community from generations, and it has been practiced through generations and such knowledge does not qualify novelty requirement for a patent [2].

Examples: agriculture methods, food production, traditional medicine, land management, ecological management, natural resource management and the like.

- Topography of Integrated circuits is non- patentable:

The topography does not fall under patent protection since it involves the arrangement of known electrical elements which are arranged in layers over a substrate which is generally made of semi-conducting material. The mere arrangement of known elements in different layers does not constitute an inventive step. A separate law is enforced to safeguard such designs or topography or layouts of the Integrated circuits [2].

2.2 Who can file the patent?

- The person who claims to be first and true inventor of an invention.

- The person being an assignee to such person who claims to be the true inventor of the invention.

- Any legal representative of the assignee or inventor who is entitled to make such an application [3].

Myth: Inventor is always an assignee of a patent.
Fact: Inventor may or may not be an assignee of a patent.

The Inventor can be an individual who involved in developing the invention whereas an assignee is a person or entity who is willing to take responsibility in legal implication of filing process and further maintaining such application after the grant.

If the inventor is a researcher, or professor, or employee then the employer of such inventor i.e., the research institute, or the university, or the company will be the assignee and applicant of such patent application.

2.3 Types of patent application

2.3.1 Ordinary application

- Provisional Application:

  A Provisional Patent Application is generally filed when your invention is still in progress and filing such provisional application will acquire a priority date. The Provisional application will not be published nor examined.

- Non-Provisional Application:

  Non- Provisional Application to be filed within 12 months from the date of filing of the provisional specification to keep the patent application in active state and such non-provisional application comprises of the detailed description which gives sufficient disclosure of the invention. Non-provisional application will be further published in respective national patent journal and examined further on request of the applicant.

- Patent of Addition or Continuation-In-Part application:

  The applicant can file a patent of addition (or Continuation-In-Part application) [4] if there is a modification or improvement of the invention which has already been applied for or patented. A patent of addition can only be granted after the grant of the parent patent.

- Divisional Application:

  Divisional application is filed if the applicant wishes to divide an application to furnish two or more applications, if the parent application claims for more than one invention. The priority date for such divisional application is similar to that of the parent application.

2.3.2 International application

- Convention Application

  A convention application is filed for claiming a priority date based on the same or substantially similar application filed in any of the convention countries. The applicant is required to file an application in their national country Patent Office within a year from the date of the initial filing of a similar application in the convention country [5].

- PCT International Application

  A PCT Application is an international application to streamline patent application process in all the member countries which are signatories to PCT with a single PCT international application. It is governed by the Patent Corporation Treaty and can be validated in 152 member countries.

- PCT National Phase Application

  A national phase application is filed in each of the country wherein the protection is sought. The national phase application must be filed within 31 months from the priority date or the international filing date, whichever is earlier [5].

Myth: PCT international application represent a universal or international patent.

Fact: A PCT application does not itself result in the grant of a patent and the grant of patent is a prerogative of each national or regional authority where the applicant decides to protect such invention.

2.4 Legal status of a patent application or a patent

Patent application and Patent are two different terms with different legal terminology. A patent application represents the filed application, and it is called as patent application until it is granted or rejected whereas, a Patent represents a granted patent application and which is renewed and maintained periodically upto to its term of 20 years.

2.4.1 Status for patent application

- Patent Application filed (Patent Pending): it determines filing of provisional or non-provisional application.

- Patent Application Published (Patent Pending): it indicates the publication of non-provisional application.

- Patent Application in examination (Patent Pending): the patent application will be examined o request by the applicant in order to put it for grant.

- Patent application in opposition (Patent Pending): this can be a pre-grant opposition applied by a third party to challenge the validity of such patent application.

- Patent Application is withdrawn: this indicates that the applicant has withdrawn the patent application from the process of grant.

2.4.2 Status for patent

- Patent Grant: determines that the patent application has been granted.

- Patent in opposition (post grant opposition): determines that the validity of such patent is challenged by an interested third party.

- Patent Lapsed: determines that the patent has been lapsed or ceased due to non- renewal of patent. Renewal of patent is mandatory to maintain the patent for the term of 20 years and renewal is paid annually.

- Patent Expired: determines that the term of patent has expired, and it falls under public domain.
- Patent Revoked: determines the revocation of patent due to non-working of such invention.

Myth: A patent application cannot be monetized until a grant is issued.

Fact: All types of patent application before grant including provisional patent applications can be licensed, sold. Although, the applicant cannot sue for infringement if such status of such patent application is pending [4].

2.5 Stages of patent filing and prosecution

2.5.1 Prior art search and filing of the patent application

The preliminary stage is to do a prior art search to valuate the novelty and inventiveness of the invention in comparison to the existing prior art and filing a patent application claiming the novelty and inventive features of the invention over the existing prior art.

2.5.2 Publication of the patent application

After the non-provisional patent application is filed by the applicant the respective patent authority will publish such application in the respective patent journal to disclose to the public. The applicant will be provided exclusive right of monetization of such invention over a limited period in exchange of disclosure of such invention to the public.

Myth: My competitors do not know about my patent application until the grant.

Fact: the patent application will be published and disclosed to public before initiating the examination process to put the application in order of grant.

2.5.3 Examination of the patent application

On request of examination from the applicant or any other interested party the patent office will proceed to examine the application to evaluate the patentability criteria and prepare an examination report stating any objection for validity of such invention.

2.5.4 Grant or dismissal of the patent application

If the objections are complied by the applicant the application will be granted else dismissed.

2.5.5 Opposition proceedings

Opposition is allowed by a third party to challenge the validity of an invention and such opposition is allowed before and after the grant of patent.

2.5.6 Infringement proceedings

If the patentee rights are exploited by a third party without the consent from the patentee, then the patentee can sue such third party for infringement of patent to claim damages for such wrongful commercial gain by the third party.

2.5.7 Working of patent or compulsory licensing

The patent granted should be worked to meet the public requirement. If such patent is not working for a certain period of time any interested third party or the government can claim compulsory licensing of such patent, wherein the third party to provide sufficient evidence stating attempts to acquire license for such invention.

2.5.8 Revocation or surrender of patent

Revocation of patent will be imposed by the governing authority if such invention is not working or not able to meet the public requirement.

2.5.9 Expiry of a patent

At the end of 20 years term, the invention protected as patent will be fall under public domain and anyone are free to use such invention even for commercial gain.

2.6 Term of the patent

All jurisdictions provide the patent a term of 20 years from the actual date of filing an application for a patent or the actual date of filing an international application under the PCT. The actual date of filing can be up to a year after the earliest priority date (In European and U.S jurisdictions).

3. Patent opposition

An opposition proceeding is an administrative process accessible under the patent law of many jurisdictions which allows any interested third parties to formally challenge the validity of a pending patent application ("pre-grant opposition"), or the granted patent ("post-grant opposition"), and such opposition can be accessed within a certain time period as defined by the respective jurisdiction. The grounds to oppose such patent application or granted patent are [6, 7]:

- Lack of novelty, lack of inventive step or such invention is not industrially applicable.
- The invention formed with a part of the prior public knowledge or the prior public use or traditional knowledge of any community.
- Invention anticipated with regard to traditional knowledge of any community, anywhere in the world.
- Ineligibility of invention (*as discussed in Section 2.1.4*)
- Wrongfully obtaining the invention.
- Insufficiency of description of the invention.
- Nondisclosure/ wrong mention of source of biological material.
- Failure to disclose information or furnishing false information relating to foreign applications filed by the applicant for the same or substantially the same.

4. Patent infringement

Patent infringement is the wrongful act committed by the infringer with respect to the exclusive rights granted to a patent holder for a patented invention. The definition of patent infringement may vary by jurisdiction, but it typically includes using for commercial gain or selling the patented invention.

Myth: If X is granted a patent, then he can claim damages against an infringer anywhere across the world.

Fact: Patents are territorial (they are effective in the country where they are granted only) and infringement is only possible in a country where a patent is in force. For example, if a patent is granted in the United States, then anyone in the United States is prohibited from making, using, selling or importing the patented item, while people in other countries may be free to exploit the patented invention in their country.

Myth: X can claim damages for patent infringement for a pending application.

Fact: X can claim damages for such patent infringement only after the grant of such patent.

4.1 What constitutes a patent infringement?

Assume Product B looks and operates like Product A, wherein Product A uses a patented invention. This does not necessarily determine that Product B is infringing the patent used in Product A. It is entirely possible that the second product uses a totally different technology to accomplish the same thing as the first product.

So, if the product or service uses all of the elements of at least one independent claim in the patent, then that constitutes an infringement.

4.2 Types of patent infringement

4.2.1 Direct infringement

Direct infringement id determined in terms of producing, utilizing, selling (or attempting to sell), or importing a protected idea or invention without obtaining authorization from the rightful owner of such patent.

Case law of direct infringement: LabCorp v. Metabolite, Inc. [8]: In 1999, Metabolite took legal action against LabCorp for infringement of a patent covering a diagnostic test. The claims of Metabolite's patent include the correlation between levels of homocysteine and vitamins B6 and B12. A jury ordered LabCorp to pay $4.7 million in damages and the choice was upheld by a federal court, which further stated that doctors were *'directly infringing' Metabolite's patents each time such a test is ordered and interpreted.'*

4.2.2 Indirect infringement

There are actually two types of indirect infringement.

- Contributory infringement, which refers to the purchasing or importing of materials that are patented, which are intended to be used as part of another patented item.

- Infringement by inducement, which refers to any activity performed by a third party that causes someone to directly infringe on a patent. Even if one of those parties is not aware of the original patent, they can still be found responsible [9].

4.2.3 Willful and literal infringement

Willful infringement involves the concept of intention. Literal infringement refers to incidents involving the exact copy of a patented item being used, sold, or imported.

4.2.4 Doctrine of equivalents infringement

If the infringing product performs the same function and yields the same results of the patented product, then it is considered as doctrine of equivalent infringement.

Case law: Graver Tank & Manufacturing Co. v. Linde Air Products Co., (1950) [10]- In this case, the Court explained that the doctrine of equivalents applies if two elements are interchangeable and a person with ordinary skill in the art would have known that the elements were interchangeable at the time of infringement.

5. Assignment and licensing of patent

Assignment of patent is transfer of ownership of the patent technology. The assignor can be the first inventor or first applicant of such patent and assignee will be the first applicant of patent application or any interested party who is capable to work such patented technology. Assignment of the patent or patent application commonly occur between the employee and the employer; student or professor and the university; or between two different corporate bodies. Such assignment depends on the respective IP policy of the respective organization.

Licensing is leasing your exclusive rights to make, sell, use to another interested party (licensee) for a limited period of time while retaining the actual patent ownership to the licensor. The types of licensing of patents or patent application are:

5.1 Exclusive license

In an Exclusive License, the licensee cannot license the patent to anyone else. It is exclusively granted to such licensee and the licensee cannot further license it to anybody else. The licensee holds the ownership of the patent for the term of the license only.

5.2 Non-exclusive license

In the non-exclusive license of the patent, the patent can be leased to more than one party, and all of them can maintain control over such patented technology to monetize the claimed product or process in such patent or patent application.

5.3 Sub licenses

Assume that the licensee needs third party contribution like requirement of work force, or certain machinery or raw materials to monetize the patented product, then the licensee can agree to sub-licensing with different organizations for the making of the product as claimed in the patent.

5.4 Cross-licensing

Assume, that two organization have their own patented technology which complement each other, then both the organizations can negotiate in terms of cross-licensing of their patented technology. Cross- licensing is required when the invention of one organization requires the support of other products or patented technology owned by the other organization to bring out the efficient product into the market.

6. Working of a patent and compulsory licensing of a patent

The granted patent or a patent application which represents an invention should be worked or atleast such patented invention to be licensed to meet the public requirement.

The non- working of the patent can pave a way for possibility of compulsory license where, an interested third party can claim a license and the governing body can allow such license without the consent of the patent holder. The royalty for such compulsory license will be estimated and awarded by the governing body itself towards the patent holder.

Landmark case of compulsory license in India is Bayer v Natco- India's first ever compulsory license was granted by the Patent Office on 9 March 2012 to Hyderabad-based Natco Pharma for the production of a generic version of Bayer's Nexavar, an anti-cancer agent used in the treatment of liver and kidney cancer.

7. Patent portfolio

Patent Portfolio represents the group of patent applications (which are filed and pending) and patents (which are granted and active) that belong to a single entity. The patent portfolio can contain hundreds, sometimes thousands, of patents.

The patent portfolio must be valuated and analyzed periodically wherein, valuation of patents can be established, and decisions can be made on such patents in terms of licensing, cross- licensing or merger and acquisitions(M&A), or technology transfer.

The Patent portfolio should me managed through IP audits which can determine the legal status of the existing patent applications and granted patents and through valuation of each application the entity can decide to maintain the most valued patents through renewals and discard such application or patents with low value either through sale or patent pooling.

Myth: Patent Portfolio with enormous number of patent applications and granted patents increase the worth of such holding entity.

Fact: The worth of patent portfolio does not depend on the number of patent application or patents, but the working of such patents determines the actual worth of the entire portfolio.

Patenting is the strategy to uplift the innovation and innovation is accomplished when such patented technology is actually practiced on industrial scale to benefit the public on large scale. If the applicant or the patentee is not capable of working the patented product or process, the best method is knowledge transfer through licensing deals to such qualified licensee or assignment (transfer of ownership) of the patent to any interested party who are capable to bring the patent technology into market to benefit the public.

The educational institutions always encounter the issue with monetization of their patent technology due to lack of sufficient infrastructure, work force, or finance as compared to industrial standards. The technology transfer is one sort of public private partnership between the educational institutions and the private sector like industries where the technology is transferred to industrial sector in return of some royalty through licensing and some other incentives like funding for research, or establishing collaborative or joint research, exchange of personnel, establishing research incubators or technology parks, training of students according to industrial norms and so on.

8. Conclusion

Patents are technology related intangible assets that drive the innovation of the technology sector. IP is a part of Innovation and patents drive such innovation. Patent terminology should be well understood by the inventors and the applicants. The Patents laws are well established in almost all jurisdictions and the corporate sector should be aware of the law to reap maximum benefits. Even, the educational institutions should be thorough with the patent system since it is the source of research. The educational institutions with standard IP policy and structure patent portfolio can involve with technology transfer agreements with corporates to reap maximum benefits for their research and even, corporates with no research department can get into such partnerships with the educational institutions to bring the invention into market to meet the public requirements.

Author details

Ojeswini Bondalapati
Registered Patent Agent of India, Hyderabad, India

*Address all correspondence to: ojeswini@gmail.com

IntechOpen

© 2021 The Author(s). Licensee IntechOpen. This chapter is distributed under the terms of the Creative Commons Attribution License (http://creativecommons.org/licenses/by/3.0), which permits unrestricted use, distribution, and reproduction in any medium, provided the original work is properly cited.

References

[1] Inventive step and non-obviousness [Internet]. 2021. Available from: https://en.wikipedia.org/wiki/Inventive_step_and_non-obviousness [Accessed: 2021-04-27]

[2] LexCampus Team, Handbook on Patent Law, The Patents act, 1970. 1st ed. LexCampus 2018. 5-6 p. DOI: 978-81-935327-0-6

[3] LexCampus Team, Handbook on Patent Law, The Patents act, 1970. 1st ed. LexCampus 2018. 7 p. DOI: 978-81-935327-0-6

[4] Vance V. Vandrake, III,ESQ, the Patent Game. 1st Ed. Legal Technology Press, U.S.A, 2019. 97-98 p. DOI: 978-0-9991144-2-1

[5] Types of patents granted and basis for rejection [Internet]. 2020. Available from: https://www.mondaq.com/india/patent/898672/types-of-patents-granted-and-basis-for-rejection [Accessed: 2021-04-27]

[6] LexCampus Team, Handbook on Patent Law, The Patents act, 1970. 1st ed. LexCampus 2018. 22-23 p. DOI: 978-81-935327-0-6

[7] Oppositions- Article 100 EPC [Internet]. 2017. Available from: https://www.epo.org/applying/european/oppositions.html [Accessed: 2021-04-27]

[8] 14 Famous Patent Infringement Cases that changed US Patent Law [Internet]. 2021. Available from: https://www.greyb.com/famous-patent-infringement-cases/ [Accessed: 2021-04-30]

[9] What Are the Different Types of Patent Infringement? [Internet]. 2019. Available from: https://bltg-ip.com/what-are-the-different-types-of-patent-infringement/ [Accessed: 2021-04-30]

[10] Doctrine of Equivalents [Internet]. 2021. Available from: https://en.wikipedia.org/wiki/Doctrine_of_equivalents [Accessed: 2021-04-30]

Section 2

Traditional Knowledge

Chapter 3

Intellectual Property Rights: Bioprospecting, Biopiracy and Protection of Traditional Knowledge - An Indian Perspective

Bency Baby T and
Timmakkondu Narasimman Kuppusami Suriyaprakash

Abstract

Patents are the form of IP most often used to seek protection of knowledge related to biological resources. The value of plants as medicinal sources is more widely recognized and the "intellectual property rights" (IPR) associated with their use and protection have been debated around the world. Indeed, being a land of indigenous cultural heritage and traditional knowledge, India is an open treasure box for whole world. IPR provisions under WIPO (World Intellectual Property Organization) and patent rights have attracted the appeal of many researchers, pharmaceutical companies and organizations to explore the potential of traditional knowledge. In this scenario, effective protection and management of Intellectual Property Rights (IPR) is essential, and India is fully committed to this. Similarly IPR and its policy framework equally contribute to development of any nation. This chapter attempts to provide information relevant to national and legal rules and policies regarding Intellectual property rights. Protection of traditional knowledge, Conservation of the rights of local and indigenous peoples to their knowledge and resources are equally important. In this regard, this chapter also discusses the concepts Biopiracy and Bioprospecting. All information is gathered from published articles and legal documents of respective countries and official websites of international organizations as these are the only sources of legal information.

Keywords: IPR, biopiracy, bioprospecting, traditional knowledge, patent

1. Introduction

Intellectual property rights include patents, trademarks, trade secrets, geographical indications and copyrights. IPR is a legal tool to protect industrial innovation in the modern world as well as to promote the protection of biodiversity and to ensure fair and equitable sharing of benefits arising from the use of genetic resources among indigenous custodians [1, 2]. Most of the patented inventions are based on previous knowledge. One of the advantages of the patent system is that it promotes further inventions on a country-by-country basis using knowledge publicly [3]. Many of the herbal products derived from traditional medicine is protected by patent laws.

Phytoconstituents have many facets in intellectual property rights (IPR) in respect of copyrights, patents, and trademark for their medicinal preparations, and registered designs [4]. The most popular forms of IP protection for herbal medicines are trade secrets and trademarks [5].

However, patenting of plant derived medicinal products and processes on the basis of knowledge gained through tradition have become a major dispute in the intellectual property rights domain [6]. Intellectual property rights in connection with indigenous knowledge have given rise to many complex legal challenges to the present world. Issues concerning the preservation of indigenous knowledge are not only legal in nature. Furthermore, the problems encountered in traditional knowledge systems due to intellectual property law can be experienced directly in communities throughout world [7].

Recently activists and some specific non-governmental organizations (NGOs) uses the term Biopiracy' to refer traditional knowledge related illegal or improper use of biological materials [8]. Furthermore, the growing number of patents also represents more exploration about biopiracy. Neem tree cases from India have shown that patents play a central role in biopiracy activity. While there has been much international discussion on disputes pertinent to intellectual property and assets, traditional knowledge and heritage, these international consultants are skeptical about the overuse of biopiracy to describe specific instances of unfair or false intellectual property claims over biological resources and traditional knowledge. Bioprospecting is a recent term constituted to describe the appropriate use of natural resources, respect the rights of indigenous peoples, and identify, commercialize bio products [3, 8–10].

However, while we protect these leading compounds and obtain private rights under the existing patent law system, the rights and interests (such as disclosure of origins, profit sharing, etc.) of the traditional knowledge owners who provide the "source" of these patents must also be respected. Otherwise, it is against the basic principles and concepts of the intellectual property system such as the interest balance [11, 12]. The Trade Related Intellectual Property Rights (TRIPS) is a key international agreement promoting the harmonization of IPR regime [13]. Key agencies like the World Intellectual Property Organization (WIPO) has also been instrumental in establishing new frameworks for the protection of Indigenous interests under intellectual property. Moreover countries at national and regional level are primarily concerned about protecting traditional resources [14]. In this regard the present chapter provides an overview of the different types of intellectual property rights and execution of legal protection of traditional resources in India. The chapter also discussed the concepts like traditional knowledge, biopiracy and bioprospecting.

2. World intellectual property organization (WIPO)

World Intellectual Property Organization (WIPO) is specialized agency of United Nations which was established in 1967, dedicated to the promotion of innovation and creativity for the economic, social and cultural development of all countries through a balanced and effective international IP system. The organization reinforces the protection of intellectual property rights, genetic resources, Folklore and Traditional Knowledge [2]. WIPO is a driving force for the international harmonization of intellectual property standards. WIPO provides a global policy forum, bringing together governments, business groups and civil society to address growing IP issues. Worldwide Protection of intellectual property and assurance of administrative cooperation among the intellectual property unions are the two main objectives of WIPO [15].

WIPO's annual study of intellectual property (IP) activities around the world is known as the World Intellectual Property Indicators. This reputable publication examines global IP activity reports. Based on 2018 filing, it covers patents, utility models, trademarks, industrial designs, microorganisms, plant variety protection and geographic indications [15]. Most international conventions pertaining to intellectual property rights are administered by the World Intellectual Property Organization. The Patent Law Treaty and the Patent Cooperation Treaty (building upon the Paris Convention for the Protection of Industrial Property) facilitate the harmonization of patent laws internationally. WIPO has played a key role in the politics and discussion surrounding IP, traditional knowledge, and biodiversity, while being disregarded by many authors and campaigners. WIPO has created a rhetorically important, but slow-moving forum in the Intergovernmental Committee on Intellectual Property and Genetic Resources, Traditional Knowledge in the realm of genetic resources and traditional knowledge (IGC) [15–17].

3. The World Trade Organization (WTO) and TRIPS

The WTO, the primary rule-making body for international trade. In order to set universal standard of protection and enforcement of IPRs among the WTO (World Trade Organization) member states, an influential international treaty came into existence which was termed as Trade-Related Aspects of Intellectual Property Rights (TRIPS). The TRIPS Agreement negotiated during the Uruguay Round of the General Agreement on Tariffs and Trade (GATT) between 1989 and 1990 and is administered by the WTO. The trade in services covered by the General Agreement on Trade in Services (GATS). These three agreements have been described as the three pillars of the WTO [18, 19]. The TRIPS Agreement aims to set minimum standards in intellectual property protection. TRIPS is considered to be the most important international agreement on IP, incorporating into it much substantive law from previous international agreements, such as the Berne Convention and Paris Convention [20]. These agreements and treaties include the General Agreement on Tariffs and Trade (GATT), the World Intellectual Property Organization (WIPO), and the Trade-related Aspects of Intellectual Property Rights (TRIPs) treaty. The main contentions in TRIPs include: patentable subject matter (for example genetically engineered products, food, medical and agricultural products, biological processes etc.), duration of protection, limitations on rights, and legal enforcement of rights [21].

4. Intellectual property rights

Intellectual property rights are the legal rights granted to a person to protect the interests of innovators and creators over their creations. It's a privilege granted to creators over their creative efforts for a set period of time [1].

There are two types of intellectual property rights:

i. Copyright and rights related to copyright

ii. Industrial property

4.1 Copyright and rights related to copyright

Copyrights are legally described term used to describe the rights of authors of literary and artistic works. Copyrights also include the rights over books and other writings, musical compositions, paintings, sculpture, computer programs and films, for a minimum period of 50 years after the death of the author. Copyright protection extends solely to expressions and does not embody concepts, procedures, and strategies of operation or mathematical ideas per se. Copyright may or may not be available for a variety of objects such as titles, slogans, or logos, reckoning on whether they contain sufficient authorship.

Under copyright, there are two categories of rights:

1. Economic rights, which allow the owner of the rights to profit financially from the utilization of their work by others; and

2. Moral rights, which protect the author's non-economic interests [1].

4.2 Industrial property

The broad application of the term "industrial property" is set out in the Paris Convention. "Industrial property shall be understood in the broadest sense and shall apply not only to industry and commerce proper, but likewise to agricultural and extractive industries and to all manufactured or natural products, for example, wines, grain, tobacco leaf, fruit, cattle, minerals, mineral waters, beer, flowers, and flour." Paris Convention – Article 1(3).

Industrial property include patents for inventions, industrial designs, trademarks, service marks, layout-designs of integrated circuits, commercial names and designations, geographical indications and protection against unfair competition [1].

4.3 Patents

Patents also referred to as patents for invention, are the most widespread means of protecting technical inventions. The term "patent", or letter "patent", also refers to the document issued by appropriate government authority. Patents are exclusive rights that are valid only in the country or territory where they were filed and granted, under the laws of that country or region.

Requirements of patentability include

- Patentable subject matter

- Industrial applicability (utility)

- Novelty

- Non-obviousness

- Disclosure of the invention.

Once a patent is granted by a state or by a regional office acting for several states, the owner of a patent has the right to prevent anyone else from commercially exploiting the invention for a limited period, generally 20 years [1, 22].

4.4 Industrial designs

Industrial designs are applied to a wide variety of industrial products and handicrafts. They refer to the ornamental or esthetic aspects of an article, including compositions of lines or colors or any three-dimensional forms that give a special appearance to a product or handicraft. In registering their industrial designs, manufacturers protect one of the creative elements that determine market success. It grants the owner of the design the exclusive right to make, import, sell, hire or offer for sale articles to which the design is applied or in which the design is embodied. The term for an industrial design rights varies from country to country. The usual maximum term is from 10 to 25 years. The layout-designs of integrated circuits are creations of the human mind [1].

4.5 Trademarks

A trademark is a distinctive indication that distinguishes certain goods or services as those produced or offered by a specific person or organization. Trademarks can be registered for both goods and services. The procedures for registering trademarks are governed by national and regional IP authorities' rules and laws. A single word, or a mix of words, letters, and numerals, will utterly represent a trademark [1, 22, 23].

4.6 Geographical indication (GI)

A geographical indication is a sign that appears on commodities that have a specific geographical origin and possess qualities or a reputation due to that place of origin. This "geographical indication" is more than just a description of the product's origin. GI indicates the connection between quality, reputation or characteristic of that good and its territory of origin. The primary role of a GI is to identify a link between a good's quality, reputation, or characteristic and its origin territory.

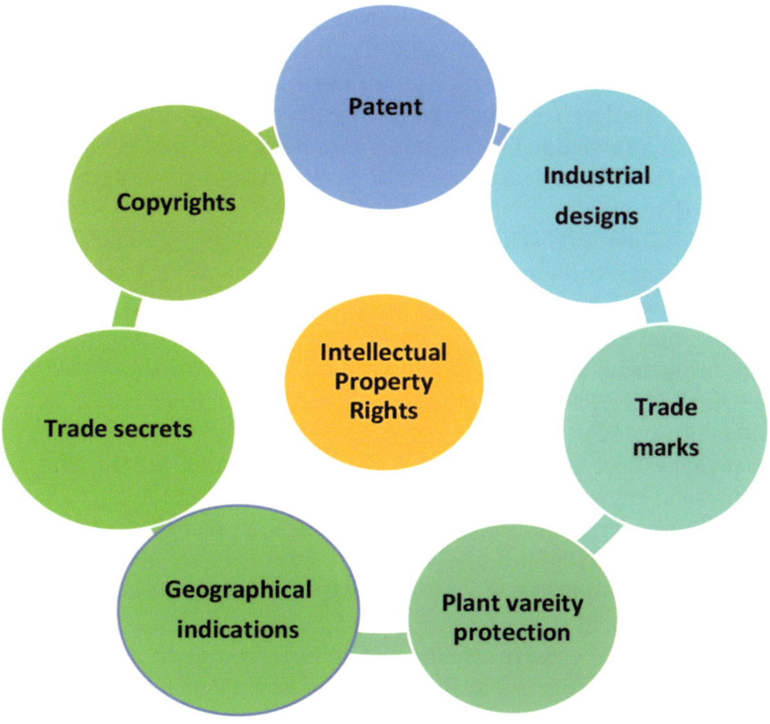

Figure 1.
Types of IPR.

Well-known examples embrace "Champagne", "Scotch Whiskey", "Tequila", and "Roquefort" cheese [1, 15, 24].

4.7 Protection against unfair competition

Protection against unfair competition supplements the protection of inventions, industrial designs, trademarks and geographical indications. It is particularly crucial for the protection of non-patentable knowledge, technology, or information that may be necessary to make the best use of a patented invention eg: The legal protection of trade secrets also part of protection of unfair competition, depending upon the legal system [1].

4.8 Plant variety protection

Plant variety protection, also known as a "plant breeder's right," is a type of intellectual property right granted to the breeder of a new plant variety in connection with certain acts relating to the exploitation of the protected variety that require the breeder's prior authorization. Prior inspection and granting by the proper authority, as in the case of patents, trademarks, and industrial designs, are required [25].

Figure 1 represents different types of intellectual property rights.

5. Traditional knowledge and intellectual property rights

Patent, copyrights, trademarks, trade secrets, geographical identification and traditional knowledge are part of IPRs [26]. The term "traditional knowledge" refers to knowledge, possessed by indigenous people, in one or more societies and in one or more forms, including, but not limited to, art, dance and music, medicines and folk remedies, folk culture, biodiversity, knowledge and protection of plant varieties, handicrafts, designs, literature (WIPO, 2011). 'It is knowledge, know-how, skills and practices that are developed, sustained and passed on from generation to generation within a community, often forming part of its cultural or spiritual identity' (WIPO, 2000). Traditional knowledge (TK) is integral to the identity of most local communities. Indigenous people, especially in rural communities, use Traditional Medicinal Knowledge (TMK) to maintain their health system [27–30].

The term traditional know-ledge can be categorized into three classes: Traditional Medicinal Knowledge (TMK), Traditional Agricultural Knowledge (TAK) and Traditional Ecological Knowledge (TEK). Indigenous knowledge is a subset of traditional knowledge category, held and used by communities, peoples and nations. Indigenous people, especially in rural communities, uses Traditional Medicinal Knowledge (TMK) maintain their health systems [30, 31].

Traditional knowledge (TK) is integral to the identity of most local communities and its preservation as such is of paramount importance for the community's social and physical environment. This knowledge is an outcome of their connection with local biodiversity that is, plants, fungi, animals, and other endemic biological materials. Traditional societies and communities are responsible for the discovery, development and preservation of a wide variety of medicinal plants, healthy herbal formulations, and agricultural and forest products that are traded internationally and generate substantial economic value. Thereby TK plays an important role in the global economy. Pharmaceutical industries have shown an interest in developing traditional medicines, from many plant species can provide important leads for the discovery of new drugs. An example is the development of the anticancer drugs vincristine and vinblastine from *Catharanthus roseous* (Apocynaceae) indigenous to Madagascar. Innovations based on TK may benefit from patent, trademark, and geographical indication protection, or be protected as a trade secret or confidential information. Traditional knowledge, on the other hand, which has ancient roots and is frequently passed down orally, is not protected by traditional intellectual property (IP) regimes. Intellectual Property (IP) rights have been claimed over biological resources and/or traditional knowledge (TK) by modifications of known properties [28, 32, 33].

However a few issues pertaining to safeguarding of traditional knowledge and traditional cultural expressions should be addressed as well [30, 31]. It is disturbing to note that keen interest have been shown by researchers from universities and large industries in indigenous plant use today for taking out the patents to profit financially, has opened up the more than hundreds of million peoples living in traditional communities around the world life in jeopardy [30, 31, 34]. While we use the existing patent law system to protect these leading compounds and secure private rights, we must also respect the rights and interests of traditional knowledge owners who offer a "source" for these patents. Moreover, potential of patent derived products from traditional medicines provides an important incentive for pharmaceutical companies, since it creates possible benefits that increase over the period of time and, thus, ultimately, for sharing such information will lead to the betterment of the mankind [35, 36].

Knowledge on indigenous plants in selected areas where the people are using for ages are many times attempted for patent provoked significant condemnation because they are based upon already existing indigenous or traditional knowledge and therefore should not meet the standard of 'new' for the patent grant. Examples of this include patents issued related to the neem tree. The European Patent Office (EPO) revoked a controversial patent on the use of antifungal agents extracted from the neem tree, it sensitize the world against biopiracy [37, 38].

Exploiting traditional knowledge resources for commercial or industrial benefits might prompt its embezzlement and can bias the interests of its legitimate custodians.

In the face of such risks, there is a need to develop ways and means to protect and nurture TK for long term development that befits the interests of Traditional knowledge-holders. The preservation, protection and promotion of the TK-based innovations and practices of local communities are particularly important for developing countries. Their rich endowment of TK and biodiversity plays an essential role in their health care, food security, culture, religion, identity, climate, trade and development [39].

According to the Summary for Policymakers of the 2019 IPBES Global Assessment on Biodiversity and Ecosystem Services:

'Recognizing the knowledge, innovations, practices, institutions and values of indigenous peoples and local communities, and ensuring their inclusion and participation in environmental governance, often enhances their quality of life and the conservation, restoration and sustainable use of nature, which is relevant to broader society. Governance, including customary institutions and management systems and co-management regimes that involve indigenous peoples and local communities, can be an effective way to safeguard nature and its contributions to people by incorporating locally attuned management systems and indigenous and local knowledge. The positive contributions of indigenous peoples and local communities to sustainability can be facilitated through national recognition of land tenure, access and resource rights in accordance with national legislation, the application of free, prior and informed consent, and improved collaboration, fair and equitable sharing of benefits arising from the use, and co-management arrangements with local communities [37, 40].

5.1 Protection of traditional knowledge

Through the Intergovernmental Committee on Genetic Resources, Traditional Knowledge and Folklore (IGC-GRTF), the World Intellectual Property Organization (WIPO) is trying to prepare a draft of an international legal instrument for protection of TK that allow access to those outside the country/community of its traditional holders. According to WIPO, Traditional knowledge is a living body of knowledge that is developed, sustained and passed on from generation to generation within a community, often forming part of its cultural or spiritual identity. WIPO's work on traditional knowledge addresses three domain areas: traditional knowledge, traditional cultural expressions and genetic resources, which are related to each other. Two types of intellectual property protection are being sought for traditional knowledge [2, 39].

5.1.1 Defensive protection

Which target to prevent people outside the community from acquiring intellectual property rights over TK. Defensive strategies might also be used to protect sacred cultural manifestations, such as sacred symbols or words from being registered as trademarks.

For example India developed a searchable database Traditional Knowledge Digital Library (TKDL) which is an evidence that treatments already used in indigenous system of medicine and ensure that patents are not granted and thus prevent the biopiracy followed by a well-known case in which the US Patent and Trademark Office granted a patent after turmeric. Defensive protection is meant to prevent piracy and application for IP as new inventions. TKDL is a prime example of a measure for defensive protection [2, 38, 39].

5.1.2 Positive protection

It empowers the communities for granting of rights to promote their traditional knowledge, control its uses and benefit from its commercial exploitation. Some uses of traditional knowledge can be protected through the existing intellectual property system, and a number of countries have also developed specific legislation [39].

6. Biopiracy

'Biopiracy' is an emergent term used to name illegal or improper appropriation of traditional knowledge and biological materials the fight against biopiracy, the preservation of biodiversity and the need for sustainable practices hence constitute one of the major challenges for the twenty-first century [30, 32]. "Natural" space of India is described through its biodiversity; a biodiversity which can be appreciated but also exploited. Bioprospecting turns into biopiracy. Vandana Shiva interpreted that, biopiracy is a phenomenon of claiming property rights to biodiversity and its products through intellectual property rights regimes and patents based on indigenous and traditional knowledge [41].

6.1 Categories of biopiracy

6.1.1 Patent-based biopiracy

The patenting of (often spurious) inventions based on biological resources and/or traditional knowledge that are extracted without adequate authorization and benefit sharing from other (usually developing) countries, indigenous or local communities [42].

6.1.2 Non-patent biopiracy

Other intellectual property control based on biological resources and/or traditional knowledge that have been extracted without adequate authorization and benefit-sharing from other (usually developing) countries, indigenous or local communities [42].

7. Bioprospecting

The emergence of the discourse of 'Bioprospecting' was discussed in (in the late 1980s or early 1990s) for the search of biological resources that can help to contribute for the conservation as well as the discovery of beneficial products [42]. Bioprospecting is defined as 'the search for biodiversity, for valuable genetic and biochemical information found in wild animals, plants or microbial organisms' for product development as a purely scientific and commercial endeavor [43]. Bioprospecting is the exploration of biodiversity for new biological resources of social and economic value. It is carried out by a wide variety of industries, the best known being the pharmaceutical industry, but also by a variety of branches of agriculture, manufacturing, engineering, construction and many others [44]. The bioprospecting concept is based on recognition of the importance of natural product discovery for the development of new crops and medicines, often based on traditional knowledge [42]. Pharmaceutical bioprospecting has been sharply criticized for what has become known as 'biopiracy' in which large international pharmaceutical corporations make use of local medicinal knowledge without acknowledging that it is indigenous intellectual property [44, 45].

Figure 2.
Kani tribe with Trichopus zeylanicus *collected from southern Western Ghats Kerala (source: The Hindu news paper dated October 18, 2012).*

However, bioprospecting has received more attention in recent years due to the increasing awareness that new drugs will be urgently needed in the near future, either to cure currently incurable diseases affecting an increasing global population or replacing increasingly ineffective drugs to treat health problems. Bioprospecting can impact any industry that depends (wholly or partly) on accessing, sourcing, processing, or production of genetic resources to develop commercially viable products for the world market [46].

An example of bioprospecting that has been cited as a success story of benefit sharing is the Kani model of access and benefit sharing (ABS). *Trichopus zeylanicus* known as 'Arogyapacha' used to treat fatigue and stress by the Kani tribe, inhabiting from Southern Western Ghat region of Kerala State in India (**Figure 2**). The lead provided by this tribal community has led to the development of a scientifically validated drug "Jeevani" by the Tropical Botanic Garden and Research Institute (TBGRI). While transferring the technology for production of the drug to the pharmaceutical firm, TBGRI agreed to share the license fee and royalty with the tribal community on a fifty-fifty basis. This is the first benefit sharing model in the world. However Kani case has criticized for whether the commercialization got informed consent from tribal community and sharing financial benefits equitably. This benefit-sharing model have been criticized for not yielding the desired the results [47–51].

8. National legislations and policies

India has a tremendous legacy of written and oral TK about elements, conservation and different applications of biodiversity for the benefit of humans, animals, and the planet. This asset of knowledge is important for preservation and human prosperity. Intellectual Property Rights is an unavoidable tool for the present globalized economy. Its more extensive use should be empowered. Notwithstanding, such utilize should not prompt the getting of Intellectual Property Rights (IPR) which cannot be advocated for something that has been made by individuals, nor can revelations made on that premise happen without recognizing the contribution of TK and sharing benefits to the makers of information fairly and equally [52]. Fostering innovation is one among the sustainable development goals set by Indian government. "An India where Intellectual Property stimulates creativity and innovation for the benefit of all" is the vision of India's National IPR Policy. Several initiatives have already proven to foster innovation like the Make in India, Start-up India, Digital India and Skill India [53]. The current laws were either enacted or revised after the TRIPS Agreement and are completely consistent with it. These laws along with various judicial decisions provide a stable and effective legal framework assurance and advancement of IPRs [54].

Systems have been planned and executed to perceive and ensure India's immense Traditional Knowledge (TK) resources. Suitable administrative and institutional components have been put in place, important plans are being carried out and funds have been set aside for this purpose. In India, institutional mechanisms and programs directly related to the use of medicinal plants are under the Ministry of Ayurveda, Yoga and Natural Therapy, Unani, Siddha and Homeopathy (AYUSH). The main legislation related to traditional knowledge is the Biological Diversity Act, 2002 and The Patents Act, 1970, build up equity in the distribution of benefits with the traditional knowledge holders and the profits derived from the use of such knowledge, and prevented improper filing of patent application for an invention based on traditional knowledge [52, 55].

8.1 India's biological diversity act, 2002

The Biological Diversity Act of 2002 (BDA) is part of an Indian law that emerged in response to compliance with the Convention on Biological Diversity (CBD), of which India is a ratified member. In fact, India has taken the lead among developing and developed nations both in introducing a substantive legislation in conformance with the objectives of the CBD. It governs the conservation of biological diversity, and sustainable utilization and equitable sharing of benefits from the use of biological resources and knowledge [53, 54]. In terms of Section 6(1) of the Biological Diversity Act, 2002 a person is prohibited from applying for any intellectual property in or outside India for any invention based on any research or information on a biological resource obtained from India, without first obtaining prior consent from the (National Biodiversity Authority) NBA. The BD Act makes admittance to TK and filling of applications for IPRs for products or invention that utilize TK, subjected to the approval of competent authorities [56–58].

8.2 The Patents act, 1970

Indian law has adequate provisions for the protection of TK and Biological Resources. The Patents Act, 1970, which defines that "invention means a new product or process involving an inventive step and capable of industrial application". Further, under Section 3(e) of the Patents Act "a substance obtained by a mere admixture resulting only in the aggregation of the properties of the components thereof or process for producing such substances" is not an invention and hence, not patentable. The Indian Patents Act also has a unique provision under Section 3(p), wherein "an invention which, in effect, is traditional knowledge or which is an aggregation or duplication of known properties of traditionally known component or components. The patents Act warrants that the subject-matter claimed in a patent application must be novel. The inventive step is another cardinal principle of patentability. Often it is said to be the final gate keeper of the patent system. The applications related to TK and/or biological material shall also be critically examined with respect to requirements of full and particular disclosure of the invention, its operation or use and the method by which it is to be performed along with the best method of performing the invention by way of working examples known to the applicant in the complete Specification as provided under Section 10(4) (a) and (b) of the Patents Act [57].

8.3 Protection of Plant Variety and Farmers' Rights Act, 2001

The Protection of Plant Varieties and Farmers' Rights Act, 2001 is a *sui generis* legislation in India providing protection for plant varieties and rights of farmers and is under the aegis of the Ministry of Agriculture. India having ratified the Agreement on Trade Related Aspects of the Intellectual Property Rights has to make provision for giving effect to agreement. To give effect to the aforesaid objectives the Protection of Plant Varieties and Farmers' Rights Act, 2001 has been enacted in India. The Act, provides a system for protection of plant varieties, farmers' and plant breeders' rights including rights in respect of their contributions made at any time in conserving, improving and making available plant genetic resources for the development of new plant varieties. It also facilitate development of seeds and their commercialization by farmers [54, 59, 60].

8.4 The National Green Tribunal Act, 2010 (NGT Act, 2010)

The National Green Tribunal is a specialized body set up under the National Green Tribunal Act, 2010 for the expeditous disposal of civil cases that are related to environmental protection, conservation of forest and other natural resources. The tribunal plays a significant role in the sustainable development of the environment [61].

8.5 Forest rights act, 2006

The Scheduled Tribes and Other Traditional Forest Dwellers (Recognition of Forest Rights) Act, 2006, was enacted to protect the rights of the forest dwelling tribal communities who had been residing in such forests for generations. The act also empowers the balance of rights with the responsibilities for sustainable use, conservation of biodiversity and maintenance of ecological balance so that forests are conserved while ensuring the livelihood and food security of the forest dwelling Scheduled Tribes and other traditional forest dwellers. Section 3(1) of the act enumerates the types of rights that the act recognizes. These include "Right of access to biodiversity and community right to intellectual property and TK related to biodiversity and cultural diversity".

The act covers rights of self-cultivation and habitation as Individual rights; and grazing, fishing and access to water bodies in forests as community rights, habitat rights for particularly vulnerable tribal groups, traditional seasonal resource access of nomadic and pastoral community, access to biodiversity, community right to intellectual property and traditional knowledge, recognition of traditional customary rights and right to protect, regenerate or conserve or manage any community forest resource for sustainable use [59, 62].

8.6 Geographical Indication of Goods (Registration and Protection) Act (1999)

The Geographical Indications of Goods (Registration and Protection) Act, 1999 is an act provide for the registration and better protection of geographical indications relating to goods. India, in compliance with its obligation under TRIPS, has taken legislative measures by enacting the Geographical Indications of Goods (Registration and Protection) Act, 1999, which came into effect on 15th September, 2003 and the Geographical Indications of Goods (Registration and Protection) Rules, 2002.

Emphasis would be laid on creating awareness regarding the rich heritage of India in terms of our Geographical Indications. As per the act "Geographical Indication", in relation to goods, means an indication which identifies such goods as agricultural goods, natural goods or manufactured goods as originating, or manufactured in the territory of a country, or a region or locality in that territory, where a given quality, reputation or other characteristic of such goods is essentially attributable to its geographical origin and in case where such goods are manufactured goods one of the activities of either the production or of processing or preparation of the goods concerned takes place in such territory, region or locality, as the case may be. Geographical indications in India include Darjeeling tea, Kancheepuram Silk, Palakkadan Matta Rice, Mysore Sandalwood Oil, Alleppey Green Cardamom, Wayanad Jeerakasala Rice etc. [15, 63].

8.7 National IPR policy

Government of India adopted the National IPR Policy in 2016, to facilitate promotion, creation and commercialization of IP assets, through a Cell for IPR Promotion and Management (CIPAM) under the aegis of Department for Promotion of Industry and Internal Trade (DPIIT) (IPR P, 2016). The national policy encourages researchers in public funded academic and R&D institutions in IPR creation by linking it with research funding and career progression. It aims to raise awareness of the value of copyright for creators, the importance of their economic and moral rights and to promote India's rich heritage of traditional knowledge with the effective involvement and participation of those knowledge holders. The main focus of this policy is related to the slogan "Creative India; Innovative India", which subsequently is aligned to different government initiatives and missions in recent times that include "Make in India", "Atal Innovation Mission", "Start Up India", and "Stand-Up India" promoting creativity, innovation and entrepreneurship in the country [57, 64, 65].

The policy suggests some measures, such as expanding the ambit of the Traditional Knowledge Digital Library (TKDL), and expanded to include other fields besides Ayurveda, Yoga, Unani and Siddha. The policy also state that traditional knowledge holders will be provided necessary support and incentives for furthering the knowledge systems that they have nurtured through civilization. The policy also seeks Activities for promotion of traditional knowledge with effective participation of holders of such knowledge. By documentation of such oral traditional knowledge will preserve the integrity of the said knowledge and traditional ways of life of the communities [54].

8.8 Traditional Knowledge digital library (TKDL)

The TKDL in India is a collaborative project between the Council of Scientific and Industrial Research (CSIR) and the Ministry of Agriculture, Food and Public Health (AYUSH). It is a nationally developed effort to ensure that patent offices around the world do not grant patents for applications based on India's ancient TK. The idea of establishing TKDL arouse as a result of India's attempt to revoke a patent granted by the United States Patent and Trademark Office (USPTO) for the wound healing properties of turmeric (*Curcuma longa*), and a patent granted by the European Patent Office (EPO) on the antifungal properties of neem (*Azadirachta indica*). Concrete measures have been taken to develop a programme aimed at documenting the knowledge and information contained in the ancient texts of Ayurveda, Siddha and Unani, as well as creating a database on the medicinal plants involved and their medical use. TKDL has transcribed more than 2.90 lakh medical formulations of Ayurveda Unani and Siddha in five internationally recognized TKDL is a collective resource in the management of intellectual property rights [52, 65].

9. International forums

9.1 The Nagoya Protocol

The Nagoya Protocol on access to Genetic Resources and the Fair and Equitable Sharing of Benefits Arising from their Utilization was adopted in Nagoya, Japan on 29 October 2010. it is a new international treaty that builds on and supports the implementation of the Convention on Biological Diversity (CBD), in particular one of its three objectives, the fair and equitable sharing of benefits arising from the utilization of genetic resources. The Nagoya Protocol is a landmark agreement in the international governance of biodiversity and is relevant for a variety of commercial and non-commercial sectors involved in the use and exchange of genetic resources. It also covers genetic resources and traditional knowledge (TK) associated with genetic resources, as well as the benefits arising from their utilization [66].

The Nagoya Protocol on Access to Genetic Resources and the Fair and Equitable Sharing of Benefits Arising from their Utilization was adopted in Nagoya, Japan on 29 October 2010. It is a new international treaty that expands on and upholds the execution of the Convention on Biological Diversity (CBD), specifically one of its three goals, the fair and equitable sharing of benefits emerging from the use of genetic resources. The Nagoya Protocol is a milestone agreement in the international governance of biodiversity. It supports various commercial and non-commercial sectors involved in the use and exchange of genetic resources. Indeed it covers genetic resources and traditional knowledge (TK) associated with genetic resources, as well as the benefits derived from their use [66].

9.2 Convention on biological diversity (CBD)

Convention on Biological Diversity (CBD) is an international treaty designed to promote sustainable development of biological diversity, conservation as well as the fair and equitable sharing of the benefits arising out of the utilization of genetic resources" CBD has been ratified by 196 nations including India. Its overall objective is to encourage actions, which will lead to a sustainable future. The Convention on Biological Diversity covers biodiversity at all levels: ecosystems, species and genetic resources [67].

10. Conclusion

Perhaps the most fundamental prerequisite for all social, economic and cultural advancement is the encouragement of intellectual creation. All branches and forms of intellectual property are therefore important, whether copyright, trademarks, industrial designs, patents or unfair competition, for the protection of traditional cultural expressions. This chapter explored briefly about the intellectual property rights with special emphasis on protection of traditional knowledge. It also discussed the overview about the concepts like biopiracy and bioprospecting. India is one of the world's most biologically and culturally diverse countries. The intellectual property law regime has seen rapid change in the last decade or so. India, a hub of TK and unique endowment has considerable unexplored potential for developing, promoting and utilizing traditional knowledge. Bioprospecting encompasses the search for the commercial potential of medicinal natural products. Consequently, it is important to deal with issues of biopiracy at the global scale. Hoping that the existing international mechanisms and national level legislations will be effective at reducing the prevalence of Biopiracy. It is the responsibilities of governments and various NGOs and corporates and the communities to nurture all forms of innovations under traditional knowledge for the benefit of mankind under the frameworks of intellectual property rights.

Conflict of interest

The authors declare no conflict of interest.

Author details

Bency Baby T[1*] and Timmakkondu Narasimman Kuppusami Suriyaprakash[2]

1 Department of Pharmacognosy, Al Shifa College of Pharmacy, Perinthalmanna, Kerala, India

2 Department of Pharmaceutics, Al Shifa College of Pharmacy, Perinthalmanna, Kerala, India

*Address all correspondence to: bencybabyt@gmail.com

IntechOpen

© 2021 The Author(s). Licensee IntechOpen. This chapter is distributed under the terms of the Creative Commons Attribution License (http://creativecommons.org/licenses/by/3.0), which permits unrestricted use, distribution, and reproduction in any medium, provided the original work is properly cited.

References

[1] WIPO 2016. Understanding Industrial Property Available from https://www.wipo.int/edocs/pubdocs/en/wipo_pub_895_2016.pdf.

[2] Javed G, Priya R, V. K. D. Protection of Traditional health Knowledge: International negotiations, National Priorities and Knowledge commons. Society and culture in south Asia. 2020;6(1):98-120. DOI:10.1177/2393861719883069.

[3] Brody BA. Traditional knowledge and intellectual property. Kennedy Inst Ethics J. 2010 Sep;20(3):231-249. DOI:10.1353/ken.2010.0003. PMID: 21133334.

[4] Singh MK, Singh SK, Singh AV, Hariom Verma H, Singh PP, Kumar A, 12 – Phytochemicals: Intellectual Property Rights, Editor(s): Bhanu Prakash, Functional and Preservative Properties of Phytochemicals, Academic Press, 2020, Pages 363-375, ISBN 9780128185933, DOI:10.1016/B978-0-12-818593-3.00012.

[5] Albert WC, Jason CL: Intellectual property protection of natural products. Asia Pacific Biotech News 8 (10):540-545. DOI:10.1142/S0219030304000862

[6] Shiva, V. (1997). Biopiracy: The plunder of nature and knowledge. 2016 ed. Berkeley, California, North Atlantic Books; 2016

[7] Anderson JE. Indigenous Knowledge and Intellectual Property Rights [Internet]. Second Edi. Vol. 11, International Encyclopedia of the Social & Behavioral Sciences: Second Edition. Elsevier; 2015. 769-778 p. Available from: DOI:10.1016/B978-0-08-097086-8.64078-3

[8] López MS, Páramo IF, The identification of biopiracy in patents. World Patent Information. 2016; 47: 67-74. DOI:10.1016/j.wpi.2016.10.003

[9] Jain A, Hallihosur S, Rangan L. Dynamics of nanotechnology patenting: An Indian scenario. Technol Soc [Internet]. 2011;33(1-2):137-44. Available from: DOI:10.1016/j.techsoc.2011.03.008

[10] Efferth T. Biopiracy of medicinal plants: Finding fair solutions for the use of natural resources. Phytomedicine [Internet]. 2019;53:294-5. Available from: DOI:10.1016/j.phymed.2018.06.047.

[11] Caplanova A. Intellectual Property, Editor(s): Fernando Pacheco-Torgal, Erik Rasmussen, Claes-Goran Granqvist, Volodymyr Ivanov, Arturas Kaklauskas, Stephen Makonin, In Woodhead Publishing Series in Civil and Structural Engineering, Start-Up Creation (Second Edition), Woodhead Publishing, 2020, Pages 81-105, ISBN 9780128199466, DOI:10.1016/B978-0-12-819946-6.00005-9.

[12] Xiaoting S. New Problems of Intellectual Property during Innovation of Traditional Chinese Medicine. World Sci Technol [Internet]. 2011;13(3):466-9. Available from: DOI:10.1016/S1876-3553(12)60014-3.

[13] Bijoy CR. Access and Benefit Sharing from the Indigenous Peoples' Perspective The TBGRI-Kani 'Model.' Law. 2007;3(1):1-19.

[14] Gupta V. An approach for establishing a Traditional Knowledge digital library. J Intellect Prop Rights. 2000;05(6):307-319.

[15] WIPO (2019). World Intellectual Property Indicators 2019. Geneva: World Intellectual Property Organization.

[16] WIPO. Summary of the Convention Establishing the World Intellectual Property Organization (WIPO Convention) 1967 available from https://www.wipo.int/treaties/en/convention/summary_wipo_convention.html.

[17] Dutfield, G. (2004) Intellectual Property, Biogenetic Resources and Traditional Knowledge, London: Earthscan Publications.

[18] Pandit D, Deb PK, Tekade RK. Patents and Other Intellectual Property Rights in Drug Delivery [Internet]. Vol. 2, Dosage Form Design Parameters. Elsevier Inc.; 2018. 705-730 p. Available from: DOI:10.1016/B978-0-12-814421-3.00020-8.

[19] Moerman L, Van Der Laan S. TRIPS and The pharmaceutical industry: Prescription for profit? Crit Perspect Account. 2006;17(8):1089-1106.

[20] Lai, J. 2014 Indigenous Cultural Heritage and Intellectual Property Rights. Cham: Springer. DOI:10.1007/978-3-319-02955-9.

[21] F.H. Erbisch FH, Maredia KM. Intellectual Property Rights in Agricultural Biotechnology. Wallingford: CAB international, 1998.4-6.

[22] WIPO. Patents. Available from https://www.wipo.int/patents/en/.

[23] WIPO 2004.Intellectual Property Handbook: Policy, Law and Use, Second Edition.

[24] Adlakha A. Case for Better GI Protection in the DDA Framework; ORIGIN Round Table on Geographical Indications, 2004 Annual WTO public symposium, 27th may 2004, Geneva.

[25] WIPO, Introduction to plant variety protection under the upov convention available from https://www.wipo.int/edocs/mdocs/sme/en/wipo_ip_bis_ge_03/wipo_ip_bis_ge_03_11-main1.pdf, updated (august 2003)

[26] Bhat SR. Innovation and intellectual property rights law—an overview of the Indian law. IIMB Manag Rev [Internet]. 2018;30(1):51-61. Available from: DOI:10.1016/j.iimb.2017.12.003.

[27] WIPO. 2011. Protecting India's Traditional Knowledge. WIPO Magazine. available from http://www.wipo.int/wipo_magazine/en/2011/03/article_0002.html(Last accessed on 11 November 2018).

[28] WIPO 2000. Traditional Knowledge. Available from. https://www.wipo.int/tk/en/tk/.

[29] Ragavan S. Protection of Traditional Knowledge. SSRN Electron J. 2005;2(2).

[30] Ahoyo CC, Houéhanou TD, Yaoïtcha AS, Prinz K, Glèlè Kakaï R, Sinsin BA, et al. Traditional medicinal knowledge of woody species across climatic zones in Benin (West Africa). J Ethnopharmacol. 2021;265(September).

[31] Van Overwalle; Protecting and sharing biodiversity and traditional knowledge: Holder and user tools, Ecological Economics 53 (2005) 585-607.

[32] Banerjee M. Biopiracy in India: Seed diversity and the scramble for knowledge. Phytomedicine [Internet]. 2019;53(July):296-301. Available from: DOI:10.1016/j.phymed.2018.10.017

[33] Sahoo N, Manchikanti P, Dey SH. Herbal drug patenting in India: IP potential. J Ethnopharmacol. 2011 Sep 1;137(1):289-297. DOI:10.1016/j.jep.2011.05.022. Epub 2011 May 27. PMID: 21640810

[34] Tedlock B. Indigenous heritage and Biopiracy in the age of intellectual

property rights. Explor J Sci Heal. 2006;2(3):256-259.

[35] Xiaoting S. New Problems of Intellectual Property during Innovation of Traditional Chinese Medicine. World Sci Technol [Internet]. 2011;13(3):466-9. Available from: DOI:10.1016/S1876-3553(12)60014-3

[36] Timmermans K. Intellectual property rights and traditional medicine: Policy dilemmas at the interface. Soc Sci Med. 2003;57(4): 745-756.

[37] IPBES (2019): Global assessment report on biodiversity and ecosystem services of the Intergovernmental Science-Policy Platform on Biodiversity and Ecosystem Services. E. S. Brondizio, J. Settele, S. Díaz, and H. T. Ngo (editors). IPBES secretariat, Bonn, Germany. XXX pages.

[38] Hellerer U, Jarayaman KS. Greens persuade Europe to revoke patent on neem tree. Nature. 2000;405(6784): 266-267.

[39] WIPO. Traditional Knowledge and Intellectual Property – Background Brief available from: https://www.wipo.int/pressroom/en/briefs/tk_ip.html.

[40] Forest Peoples Programme, International Indigenous Forum on Biodivversity, Indigenous Women's Biodiversity Network, Centres of Distintion on Indigenous and Local Knowledge, Secretariat of the Convention on Biological Diversity. Local Biodiversity Outlooks 2: The contributions of Indigenous Peoples and local communities to the implementation of the Strategic Plan for Biodiversity 2011-2020 [Internet]. 2020. Available from: www.localbiodiversityoutlooks.net

[41] Shiva V. Recovering biodiversity. Soc Change. 2001;31(1-2):21-37.

[42] Robinson DF. Biopiracy and the innovations of Indigenous peoples and local communities. Indig Peoples' Innov Intellect Prop Pathways to Dev. 2012; 77-93.

[43] Priya R, Kurian CM. Regulating Access and Protecting Traditional health Knowledge through intellectual property rights? Issues from a holistic health systems perspective. Sci Technol Soc. 2018;23(3):504-529.

[44] Beattie AJ, Hay M, Magnusson B, de Nys R, Smeathers J, Vincent JFV. Ecology and bioprospecting. Austral Ecol. 2011;36(3):341-356.

[45] Mgbeoji, Ikechi. (2006). Global Biopiracy: Patents, Plants, and Indigenous University of British Columbia Press, 2006.

[46] Resource Manual for Bioprospecting. available from. http://ipbio.org/pdfs/papers/ResourceManual_Oct14_2004.pdf.

[47] The Hindu. A benefit-sharing model that did not yield desired results. 2012. available from. https://www.thehindu.com/news/national/A-benefit-sharing-model-that-did-not-yield-desired-results/article12561312.ece.

[48] TBGRI Model of Benefit Sharing. http://www.kerenvis.nic.in/Database/TBGRI_1402.aspx. Last Updated: 23/02/2021

[49] WIPO. Using Traditional Knowledge to Revive the Body and a Community. available from https://www.wipo.int/ipadvantage/en/details.jsp?id=2599.

[50] Shiva V. Bioprospecting as sophisticated Biopiracy. Journal of Women in Culture and Society. 2007; 32: 307-313 DOI:10.1086/508502

[51] Chaturvedi S. ABS and Kani Case in India. 2008;1-36.

[52] UNEP. The Clearing-House Mechanism of the Convention on Biological Diversity: 6th National Report-India. 2018;1-270. Available from: https://chm.cbd.int/database/record?documentID=245938.

[53] Patents. Available from. https://ipindia.gov.in/vision-patent.htm.

[54] National-IPR-Policy. 2016. available from https://dipp.gov.in/sites/default/files/national-IPR-Policy20114October 2020.pd.

[55] Mitra A. India: Biological Diversity Act, 2002 and Patenting of Biological Inventions In India – Part I (Section – 6). 2017. https://www.mondaq.com/india/patent/589566/biological-diversity-act-2002-and-patenting-of-biological-inventions-in-india-part-i-section-6

[56] Government of India, The Biological Diversity Act, 2002. INDIA CODE Digital Repository of All Central and State Acts. 2002;1-20. Available from: http://www.nbaindia.org/act/act_english.htm.

[57] Guidelines for processing of patent applications relating to traditional Knowledge and biological material. 2005. available from http://www.ipindia.gov.in/writereaddata/Portal/IPOGuidelinesManuals/1_39_1_5-tk guidelines.pdf.

[58] NBAP. India's National Biodiversity Action Plan An Overview – 2019. 2019;198. Available from: https://www.cbd.int/doc/world/in/in-nbsap-other-en.pdf.

[59] Protection of plant varieties and farmers' rights authority, India, available from http://www.plantauthority.gov.in/about-authority.htm.

[60] The Gazette of India PART II – Section 1. The protection of plant varieties and farmers' rights act, 2001. 2001;(Dl):1-50.

[61] Government of India. The National Green Tribunal Act, 2010. 2014;1-19.

[62] Forest Rights Act. Govt of India. available from https://tribal.nic.in/FRA.aspx.

[63] Sharma A. India: Geographical Indication Tagging Of Agricultural Products and Foodstuffs. Available from https://www.mondaq.com/india/trademark/898690/geographical-indication-tagging-of-agricultural-products.

[64] Verma D, Governance G. National Intellectual Property Rights Policy of India – A Review AWARENESS ABOUT INTELLECTUAL Editors Dr Anita Moudgil DAV College for Girls Yamunanagar National Press Associates, New Delhi. 2020;(July).

[65] Gaudillière JP. An indian path to biocapital? The traditional knowledge digital library, drug patents, and the reformulation regime of contemporary ayurveda. East Asian Sci Technol Soc. 2014;8(4):391-415.

[66] Factsheets. Introduction to Access Introduction to access and benefit-sharing. CBD. Convention on Biological Diversity.2011;1-6.

[67] The Convention on Biological Diversity, available from https://www.cbd.int/intro/

Chapter 4

Harnessing Traditional Knowledge Holders' Institutions in Realising Sustainable Development Goals in Kenya

Francis Kariuki

Abstract

The paper examines the role of traditional knowledge (TK) holders' institutions in the realisation of components of Sustainable Development Goals (SDGs)-9 and 16. Using two case studies, from the kaya elders (Mijikenda community) and Mbeere traditional potters, the study found that TK holders' institutions are essential, and can play pivotal roles in attaining aspects of the said SDGs. As key drivers of, and essential governance frameworks for innovation, they contribute to the creation, diffusion and application of innovation (a component of SDG 9); while the innovation they generate continues to replenish and strengthen them. Additionally, their role in promoting peace and justice, and an inclusive and practical approach to gender means that they can be instrumental in strengthening formal institutions, especially the intellectual property (IP) institutions (a component of SDG 16). As data repositories and governance frameworks, they have an impact on the prevalence, type and nature of entrepreneurial activities that TK holders can engage in.

Keywords: traditional knowledge holders' institutions, sustainable development goals, traditional knowledge, traditional knowledge holders' innovation, entrepreneurship, data

1. Introduction

Traditional institutions encompass different types of Indigenous organisations that differ based on their functions such as local governance, community resource mobilisation, security, asset management, conflict resolution, management committees for infrastructure and sector services, among others [1]. They are complex and multifaceted and have been typologised into land-based, livestock-based, labour-sharing, mutual assistance (social), health, traditional beliefs (including rituals, spiritual leaders & sacred areas), traditional leaders, recreational, and conflict resolution institutions [2].

The study conceptualises traditional knowledge (TK) holders' institutions [3] broadly, as socially embedded, flexible, legitimate, inclusive and holistic frameworks with regulatory, cognitive and normative dimensions, making them a valuable resource for achieving SDGs [4–6]. They encompass the laws, customs,

IntechOpen

traditions, social networks and entities (including councils of elders and certain individuals holding specialised knowledge).

The study focuses on SDGs-9 and 16. SDG-9 deals with industries, innovation, and infrastructure [7], while SDG-16 focuses on peaceful and inclusive societies, access to justice and the building of strong institutions [8]. The study focuses on SDG-9 because TK holders' institutions have a role in the promotion of innovation. Whereas most studies have focused on the interplay between IP institutions and innovation, there is less focus on the role of TK holders' institutions in promoting innovation. Analysing TK holders' institutions, will shed light on their role in driving innovation, and addressing institutional barriers (e.g. failure to meet the test of rigidly established industrial standards within IP rights) to the commercialisation of innovations by communities and realisation of their entrepreneurial potential [9]. Moreover, and while IP institutions have been criticised for being gender biased against women innovators and creators [10], local institutions 'may feature more or less restrictive gender norms' and hence create opportunities for the different groups to participate in, and benefit from innovation processes [11, 12]. The case studies in this work will illuminate on the gender dimension of TK holder's innovation, and the inclusive and practical approach to gender of TK holders' institutions.

Promoting SDG-16 holds the promise for building institutions to promote justice and empower TK holders, most of whom are living in abject poverty yet their TK and associated resources continue to be misappropriated through the IP regime. It, therefore, becomes necessary to evaluate the role of TK holders' institutions in strengthening formal institutions such as the IP institutions.

Relatedly, due to the data generated by TK holders' institutions, and their role in driving innovation, they provide a conducive environment for entrepreneurship, and determine prevalence, type and nature of entrepreneurship. This is particularly true in Africa where most goods and services are sourced, produced and sold within families or other trusted social networks in a collaborative manner ([6], note 4 at 95).

Moreover, TK holders' institutions are data repositories and data governance frameworks that can be deployed in designing a strong regime for TK holders' data sovereignty. The data they hold underlies their innovative capacity; strengthens institutions; manages, monitors and mitigates risks; and thus hold the promise for the realisation of the developmental needs and aspirations of TK holders including the attainment of other SDGs such as SDG-15 [13] and 13 [14].

The paper has six sections. Section 1 is this introduction that sets out the general outline of the study. Section 2 discusses the methodology. In Section 3, the two case studies are discussed to set the research context. The broad conceptual parameters are set out in Section 4, where TK holders' institutions are discussed. It then situates TK holders' innovation within the wider framework of innovation. It then discusses TK holders' institutions, and their contribution in strengthening formal institutions such as the IP institutions. Thereafter, the study conceptualises TK holders' institutions, and their role in driving entrepreneurship, and in data governance. Section 5 sets out the findings of the study thematically including the challenges bedevilling the TK holders' institutions while Section 6 is the conclusion.

2. Research methodology

The research was a desktop study supplemented by semi-structured interviews and focus group discussions (FGDs) in the two case studies [15]. The Mbeere community was selected because of its traditional pottery practices while the Mijikenda community was selected because of their effective form of traditional management systems of the *kaya* forests (sacred groves). In the Mijikenda case study, I built upon previous research that I carried out as part of my doctoral project in 2018 on the role of traditional institutions in the protection of TK. Through that study, I was able to establish close personal, professional relations and mutual trust with the community, allowing easy access to information. Thus, it was easy to identify the respondents to participate in the interviews and FGDs.

The findings are based on 25 interviews conducted in the 2 case studies mainly with TK holders' representatives, researchers, civil society organisations (CSOs) and government agencies. I contacted some of the interviewees via phone especially those from CSOs and government agencies that I had interviewed previously in the course of the doctoral project. The interviews were conducted between 14/10/2019 and 05/11/2019. Among the Mijikenda, I interviewed 15 people. 10 of the interviews were *kaya* elders, 2 members of CSOs working in the area (Community Action for Nature Conservation (CANCO), and Trust for Indigenous Culture and Health (TICAH)), and 3 government representatives (Kenya Forest Service (KFS), Coastal Forest Conservation Unit (CFCU) and Kenya Resource Center for Indigenous Knowledge (KENRIK) based at the National Museum of Kenya (NMK).

In the Mbeere case study, I interviewed 10 people. Majority of the interviewees were women involved in pottery [8] and 4 from CSOs (African Biodiversity Network (ABN) and the Institute for Culture and Health (ICE). The length of the semi-structured interviews ranged from 30 minutes to one hour and 15 minutes, on average lasting approximately 45 minutes, where questions focused on the role of TK holders' institutions in the promotion of innovation and building of strong institutions. Both closed and open-ended questions were used to ensure comprehensive coverage of the issues, and to minimise the disadvantages arising from using only one form of questioning, while maximising the advantages of each. The interviews allowed respondents to express views in their own terms and in detail. Purposive selection was used to identify the key informants.

To complement the interviews and to verify some of the claims made during the interviews, 2 FGDs were organised with key informants identified during the interview process. One in Kaloleni in Kilifi on 4 November 2019 for the *kaya* elders, and another in Ishiara on 12 November 2019 for the Mbeere. Each of the FGDs lasted approximately 45 minutes. There were 15 people in the Mijikenda FGD comprising mostly *kaya* elders, community members, county forest guards, representatives from National Museum of Kenya (NMK), and the Coastal Forest Conservation Unit (CFCU). In the Mbeere case study, the FGD comprised of 10 potters since there are currently no efforts by government or CSOs to support the potters. The purpose of the FGDs was to obtain information from informants on how TK holders' institutions can be harnessed to realise innovation and strengthen institutions. Moreover, through the FGDs, the researcher gained insights into the data that TK holders' institutions generate, their role in data governance and entrepreneurship.

The interviews, FGDs and literature review were structured so as to answer the following questions. What are the existing TK holders' institutions with the potential to contribute to innovation and strong institutions in Kenya? How can TK holders' institutions be harnessed in the realisation of innovation and strong institutions in Kenya? What role do women play in driving innovation, and in relation to TK holders' institutions? What data do TK holders' institutions generate and how does the said data strengthen those institutions and innovation, and thus boost the SDGs? And what role can TK holders' institutions play in data governance to engender transformational entrepreneurial potential for TK holders?

The qualitative data gathered from the semi-structured interviews and FGDs was analysed using a thematic deductive analysis approach. This approach aided in the identification of themes and interpretation of information. The interviews were recorded and transcribed, while notes were taken from the FGDs. Transcripts were reviewed and systematically coded using a coding grid. The common codes in the grid were then interlinked to highlight similarities and differences within and between the codes. Selected codes were consolidated and given a descriptive label in order to reflect a specific theme bearing in mind the research questions. The themes were then reviewed and refined to eliminate coding redundancies, and to ensure the data is accurately portrayed. Thereafter, the themes were defined, named and those reflecting a similar idea merged into global themes, and inserted in a column within the coding grid. Interpretation was done by identifying and examining the underlying ideas, assumptions, conceptualisations and ideologies that shape or inform the data, bearing in mind the research questions. Lastly, the research project was written up in a way that illustrates the trustworthiness and validity of the results, relating analytically the experiences from the three case studies, and linking them to relevant literature. The broad themes that rose from the data are: existence and nature of TK holders' institutions and the roles of TK holders' institutions in: innovation, building strong institutions, entrepreneurship and data governance.

3. Research context

3.1 The Mijikenda, *kaya* elders and their TK practices

The first case study relates to the *kaya* forests, the sacred forests of the Mijikenda, a Bantu-speaking people consisting of nine sub-communities namely: the *Chonyi, Digo, Duruma, Giriama, Jibana, Kambe, Kauma, Rabai* and *Ribe* who are closely related linguistically and culturally [16]. The name Mijikenda is a Swahili derivative from the expression *midzi chenda* (nine homes) referring to the nine constituent sub-communities. According to historians, the Mijikenda migrated into the coastal area in the 16th century or earlier from a northern homeland known as Singwaya or Shungwaya [17]. When they migrated into Kenya, they settled in fortified hilltop villages known as *kaya* (meaning a settlement, village or home) as they were at risk of attack from other communities [18]. Each Mijikenda sub-community has its own *kaya*, which is a political institution and a settlement with a closely-knit society controlled by a council of elders, the *kambi* or *ngambi* ([16], note 14 at 4). Each *kaya* has its own history, committee of elders, and set of environmental and socio-cultural circumstances; but there are common themes traceable among them [19]. Currently, there are about 60 *kaya* forests, covering an area of about 4000 acres and representing 'some of the few patches of undisturbed vegetation in an increasingly densely-populated landscape' ([18], note 16 at 15). Today, the Mijikenda are found in Kilifi, Kwale and Mombasa counties. There are however no *kayas* in Mombasa County. Kwale County is home to the Digo and Duruma sub-communities while Kilifi County has the other 7 Mijikenda sub-communities. The study focused on Kilifi County since it has some of the best-managed *kayas* and there is strong adherence to cultural traditions. Moreover, most of the Kilifi *kayas* are on the World Heritage listing whereas in Kwale it is only the Duruma *kayas* that are listed (**Figures 1** and **2**).

Over time, the *kaya* elders have developed a system for protecting their TK and forests. Under that system, the elders are viewed as custodians, with the

Figure 1.
An image of kaya Kauma in Kilifi County. It is listed as a world heritage site.

Figure 2.
An image of kaya Kambe in Kilifi County. It is also listed as a world heritage site.

responsibility for regulating access, use and control of resources (including TK) in accordance with customary laws (including rites and taboos) and enforcing them. Through taboos, for instance, they regulate who can access the forests, when, how and for what reasons. For example, it is a taboo to enter; bring flames; fence; or cut trees in the *kaya* without the consent of the elders [20].

Moreover, TK is held at the individual, family/clan or community levels. Individuals may hold specialised knowledge on the use of specific plants and carving of *vigango* (memorial statues erected on tombs), which means it is their prerogative to share it [21]. TK relating to spiritual healing is viewed as family/clan property, and is selectively inherited either before or after the life of a practising healer, or spiritually guided, where a selected heir falls sick until he takes up the practice

([16], note 14 at 13-14). At the community level, certain rituals/ceremonies are conducted by initiated elders for community benefit including: prayers in times of drought or famine; cleansing of land; thanksgiving prayers and blessing of the harvest; prayers for healing community members; prayers for peace; and divination [22].

Apart from holding TK, and conserving the *kaya* forests, the elders play a key role in promoting unity, conflict resolution, rule-making, and enforcement of those rules [22]. The elders and forests are a symbol of unity and cultural identity for the Mijikenda people [23]. Moreover, elders are the first port of call wherever there are disputes (including land, family and political) in the community. Further, local politicians, must seek the blessings of the *kaya* elders, before venturing into politics, illustrating their acceptance and legitimacy (**Figure 3**) [22].

There are collaborations between *kaya* elders and governmental and non-governmental agencies to protect their TK and resources [23]. For example, some *kaya* forests are World Heritage Sites [24] and are under the management of the NMK and the stewardship of United Nations Educational, Scientific and Cultural Organisation (UNESCO). Additionally, NMK in collaboration with UNESCO and the State Department of Culture runs a program aimed at recognising the intangible cultural heritage (ICH) in the *kayas* and the recognition of secondary *kayas*, in need of urgent protection from extinction [21]. Moreover, CFCU is working with *kaya* elders to sensitise the youth on the cultural and ecological value of forests (through essay competitions, visits to schools, and field trips); strengthen traditional institutions; support elders in fencing some forests; and recruit guards to monitor the forests and report any infraction of regulations to the elders ([18], note 16 at 23). Similarly, the County Government of Kilifi, has established the County Forest Guards who work with elders to prevent encroachment into the forests. TICAH, a local NGO, has a program on TK and culture, where it is working with elders to document their TK, rituals and traditions. In particular, TICAH is working to document and commercialise TK relating to medicine [25].

Figure 3.
The researcher (holding a cap) attended a customary court session on 26th April 2018 at Mwembe Marunga where Rabai elders sit (under a mango tree) to hear and determine disputes touching on land, adultery, witchcraft, marital and family disputes every Monday and Wednesday among locals.

3.2 The Mbeere and their traditional pottery practices

This study focused on pottery among the Mbeere people, in Ishiara area. Ishiara is famous for traditional pottery, and has a market for pots. Pottery is done by women (mothers and grandmothers) who pass on those skills to their daughters as they grow up. They practise pottery on a part-time basis and seasonally since most potting takes place during the dry season (August) after harvesting, when the potters have time to spare. Thus, pottery helps women supplement their income, and mitigate against food shortages in their families [26].

The pots are used for various purposes such as cooking vessels, as hearths, *jiko* (cooker) linings, storage equipment and flower vases. Food prepared using the pots is tastier than that prepared using aluminium vessels [26]. Moreover, the pores in the clay helps filter dirt from water hence making it relatively clean and safe for drinking. Additionally, since Mbeere is an arid and semi-arid area, and temperatures can rise upto 40 degrees, the community uses the pots to cool drinking water. Further, the pots retain more heat than normal cooking pots thus conserving firewood [26].

Pottery making goes through the following processes: procurement of raw materials, preparation of the clay, forming the vessels, surface treatment, decoration, drying and firing [27]. The raw materials used are red-brown clay (from a place called *Cianthugi)*, water and fire. Potters prefer clay derived from weathered rocks as it has small particle sizes and plate-like characteristics, and other chemical properties that allow it to be worked into shape and baked, to create the vessels ([27], at 36). Preparation of the clay entails removing any organic and inorganic impurities which may crack the pot while drying. It is then finely ground, mixed with water and treaded before kneading to improve plasticity and remove air bubbles. Thereafter, the process of forming/shaping the pots begins, which entails coming up with flattened coils out of the kneaded clay that are joined together to form a circular structure as shown in **Figure 4**. Surface treatment/finishing helps to remove impurities/marks left while forming/shaping the pot such as finger depressions [27].

Figure 4.
A potter engaged in pot forming.

Where decorations are necessary, they are incised using a piece of stick or a broken piece of calabash (**Figures 5** and **6**). The decorations consist of simple horizontal rows of dots/lines, grooved horizontal zigzag or wavy lines confined to

Figure 5.
Grooves and dots decorations.

Figure 6.
Zigzag line decoration on a pot.

or just below the neck of the pot [27]. Decorations are also applied using different colours especially for pots meant for use as flower vases, see **Figures** 7 and **8**.

Thereafter, the vessel is dried under a shade, away from direct sunlight for about 5 days to remove water that is mechanically combined with clay particles [26]. Direct sunlight is avoided since rapid drying due to high temperatures can cause cracks. After the initial drying, the pot is dried directly under the sun. The duration for direct drying varies depending on the size and relative humidity. When dry, the pots are baked hard by firing them under high temperatures. To ensure even and/or controlled firing, firing is usually done late in the evening when the wind is not blowing. Thereafter, they allow the pots to cool before

Figure 7.
A flower vase decorated using black and white colour paint.

Figure 8.
Colour decorations on a pot meant for use either as a flower vase or a house decoration.

pulling them out from the fire using tongs thus preventing cracking through rapid heat loss. Once ready, the women hawk the pots around the village or take them to Ishiara market (**Figure 9**) [27].

The vessels may also have different shapes. There are wide-mouthed pots (mostly for cooking); narrow-mouthed (for storing water and grains); and with

Figure 9.
Pots for sale at Ishiara market.

varying basal shapes-flat bases (used as flower vases) and rounded/cylindrical bases (for cooking) (**Figures 10** and **11**) [27].

Figure 10.
Wide-mouthed pots.

Figure 11.
Pots with a rounded or cylindrical bases.

4. Conceptual context

4.1 TK holders' institutions

TK holders' institutions are complex, multifaceted governance frameworks that deal with diverse subject matters, depending on their functions, to wit: land, livestock, labour-sharing, mutual assistance (social), health, traditional beliefs (including rituals, spiritual leaders & sacred areas), traditional leadership, recreational, and conflict resolution ([2], note 2 at 111). They include customary laws and practices; family secrets; oral agreements; sharing mechanisms; community sanctions; trust; and ostracism [28, 29]. They have remained resilient, and enjoy popular legitimacy because of their 'proximity and intimate familiarity with their communities' which makes them 'more effective in adjudicating disputes, allocating land, and advocating for their constituents than many MPs, local councillors, and state institutions' [30]. The legitimacy also stems from the fact that they function according to cultural norms which people are deeply familiar with, thus facilitating both access and (non-electoral) accountability [30–32], especially where formal state institutions have failed or had limited access. This is in consonance with studies suggesting that 'successful engagement with rural communities should start with recognising that they have institutions through which they can practise or organise collective action' ([2], note 2 at 2). A study conducted on the Mijikenda, confirms that 'respect for the indigenous institutions remains strong' in the community ([23], note 25 at 327-350).

As governance frameworks for TK and natural resources, and data repositories (holding knowledge, social networks, ethos, values, methods of utilising resources and conservation etc.) ([4], note 4 at 6). They are also custodial institutions that aim at 'the continuous use and preservation of the place, its values, and its surrounding environment, including the preservation of its symbolic and cosmological significance' ([4], at 107).

TK holders' institutions generate social capital-binding and bridging social capital-that is considered 'an additional factor of production' [33]. Social capital (social norms, relationships and networks) can be mobilised to address societal challenges, create positive synergies, and ensure efficient use of resources since 'people who share a common background, language, culture, and customs' are able to mobilise resources effectively ([1], note 1 at 4). Social networks allow the formation of linkages between local knowledge and formal sciences that can have positive impacts in society [34, 35].

Withal, local institutions have been conceptualised within a broader set of theories of institutions, where the aim is to 'get institutions right' and/or strengthen institutions ([5], note 4 at 290), [36, 37]. This approach is informed by various factors. First, there is a prevailing view that good governance, strong and accountable institutions are crucial for poverty reduction and development effectiveness [38]. Second, the massive failure of formal state institutions to project their authority, especially in rural contexts, has produced a development agenda fixated on building institutional capacity [39, 40].

Consequently, the inordinate focus on formal institutions, for instance, in the context of TK protection, means that great efforts have been dedicated towards harnessing the IP regime to protect TK rather than on TK holders' institutions. Moreover, overemphasis on formal institutions, has resulted in a negative attitude towards traditional institutions. They have been highly criticised, *inter alia,* for being prone to manipulation by powerful forces in the community, gender bias, and abuse of power [41]. Such criticism, for instance that the institutions have a gender bias, is at times misplaced, since as this study shows, the roles of men and women are clearly recognised in those institutions. This limits the extent to which they can be deployed in encouraging innovation, building strong institutions and promoting entrepreneurship.

Despite the focus on formal institutions, the use of some of those institutions, like the IP regime to protect TK holders' innovations, faces certain technical and practical challenges. For instance, TK and TK based innovation may not meet the necessary criteria for IP protection. Besides, the sort of exclusive rights granted through formal IP protection cannot offer the necessary protection and appropriation to TK holders' innovations, which are mostly developed collectively. In the TK context, non-pecuniary incentives (intrinsic motivation) plays a considerable role in driving innovative behaviour unlike with IP where the 'prospects of exclusivity and financial rewards' are the main incentives ([28], note 43 at 242). Further, the use of the IP system by TK holders is constrained by low levels of awareness of IP, challenges in accessing IP protection measures, lack of technical expertise/personnel and financial resources, low investments in R&D, high cost of filing and challenging enforcement, and inadequate administrative infrastructure ([28], at 237).

Nonetheless, TK holders' can, for instance, use the IP system (such as patent, trademark, geographical indications, or trade secret or confidential information) to: protect their innovation against unauthorised usage of protected IP by competitors; help commercialise IP-protected products and services; help licence inventions and create corresponding technology markets; increase brand-based enterprise recognition; signal to potential venture capital to obtain business finance; limit the right of employees to enter employment with competitors; ensure that information is kept confidential; ensure the transfer of rights related to inventions from employees to companies; and facilitate sharing of rights in the results of cooperative projects in a manner that satisfies all contracting parties ([28], at 236). Indeed, IP becomes more important as interaction between the informal and formal sectors for joint collaborative innovation increases ([28], at 240). Sometimes, too, innovation in the informal sector occurs with the help of formal sector scientific institutions, and vice versa [42] hence the need for the much-developed IP system in protecting the ensuing innovation.

4.2 TK holders' institutions and innovation

An innovation is defined as 'the implementation of a new or significantly improved product (good or service), or process, a new marketing method, or a new organisational method in business practices, workplace organisation or external relations' [43]. In this context, innovative activities include 'the acquisition of machinery, equipment, software and licences, engineering and development work, design, training, marketing and R&D where undertaken to develop and/or implement a product or process innovation' [43]. The motivation for innovation includes the desire to increase market share, enter new markets, improve product range, increase the capacity to produce new goods, reduce costs and so on [44], ([42], note 61 at 54). In the formal sector, markets are recognised as one of the main drivers of innovation. In the context of TK holders, formal markets may not exist [45], as communities might be interested in non-market transactions such as sharing a product rather than taking it to the market to increase market share.

Institutions play a key role in driving innovations, and are one of the five building blocks of innovation systems [46]. Institutions determine the speed, magnitude and quality of innovation processes ([12], note 18 at 6), manage uncertainty, provide information, manage conflicts, promote trust among groups, diffuse innovations, and mediate distributional effects of innovation processes related to social class, gender, age, ethnicity, or political power ([12], at 7). They also provide incentives for learning, knowledge and innovation production ([46], note 66 at 56).

TK holders' institutions play a critical role in driving TK holders' innovation and innovation processes. TK holders' innovations are part of, and are a by-product of TK since TK entails 'knowledge, know-how, innovations, skills and practices' [47, 48] of local communities. Indeed, the innovation process has been conceptualised as one where 'knowledge' is both 'an input and output' since innovations 'reflect the introduction of a new combination of existing knowledge into the economy, and the innovation itself represents new knowledge' [49].

Social capital among TK holders' spurs and enhances innovation ([34], note 52 at 1), ([35], note 52 at 16-18) by facilitating access to resource (contacts, markets, credit and diverse domains of knowledge), and plays a critical role not only in the generation and diffusion of innovation ([33], note 50). Bridging social capital allows TK holders to increase their innovative capacity, meet social goals and expand institutional networks at local level and beyond, as they interact with actors such as financial institutions, development agencies, political elites in the community, and technical experts (including researchers and extension staff) in order to advance their innovation processes ([33], at 1), ([34], note 52 at 1), [50]. Hence, their institutions are useful in bridging the gap between the formal and informal institutions. Conversely, innovation processes contribute to building social capital, both bonding capital (intra-group) and bridging capital (inter-group) within local communities.

Indeed, what makes social capital a vital ingredient to the innovative process is the fact that it 'reduces certain costs like information sharing, transaction costs and enforcement costs and this leaves many resources available for use for innovation-related expenditure' ([34], at 36). In rural areas, the diffusion of innovation can greatly benefit from the involvement of women since they play a central role in building social networks that are the main media through which new products or services, commercial or otherwise, are proposed, deliberated and accepted or rejected [51]. However, in the context of small firms, strong social capital could be a liability as well as an asset. Sometimes, dense networks might inhibit 'innovative practices and new ideas' while other times absence of ties is said to promote the generation of new ideas and knowledge. Weak ties may also play an important role in bridging the gap between the formal and informal institutions ([33], note 50). However, with TK holders' institutions, the existence of dense networks might not inhibit innovation since there are customary laws that act as normative frameworks, governing the rights and obligations of community members at the individual, clan, family and community levels.

Studies suggest that innovation is occurring in the informal economy ([28], note 43), ([34], note 52 at 2), ([50], note 74) 'in a new set of under-studied contexts', ([42], note 61), [52], ([53], note 79) some of which are relevant to TK holders. One of these contexts is innovation in community-based settings, such as homes, villages, craft workshops and among informal and semi-formal networks [53]. Innovation activities in these contexts are 'extremely diverse, as are the sources of knowledge, learning and innovation that shape and diffuse them' ([42], note 61 at 63). Those innovations are described variously as grassroots, informal, rural, pro-poor, frugal or *jugaad,* local, social, endogenous innovation ([12], note 9 at 9), ([52], note 79), [51, 54]. A discussion of all these innovations is clearly beyond the scope of this study. However, some of these forms of innovation are relevant to TK holders' innovation, as they tend to go beyond enterprise innovation and typical firm incentives to innovate (such as increased revenue and market share) ([44], note 64 at 345). Moreover, such innovations incorporate knowledge domains beyond science, engineering and technology, by paying more attention to innovation metrics that capture spontaneous, process-based, and needs-driven innovations on the demand-side of the economy ([29], note 43 at 4), as discussed below.

Social innovation refers to innovations and processes of innovation that are social in nature (such as networking, collaboration, group formation, organisational governance and management practices), that improve a society's ability to create opportunities for investment, growth and development [55, 56]. Social innovation recognises that innovations can emerge through self-organisation, self-empowerment and development ([54], note 82 at 5), making it particularly relevant to TK holders who have unique institutions for self-governance, and who hold their TK collectively, and at times for certain social purposes, such as environmental conservation. Pro-poor innovation is relevant to TK holders due to their poor social and economic conditions. Inclusive innovation, *inter alia*, seeks to, ensure the inclusion of all the necessary stakeholders (including the excluded population) in the design, development, and in defining the problems and solutions that an innovation seeks to address ([44], note 64 at 345), [57]. Therefore, inclusive innovation is apposite to TK holders, and women as it eschews the exclusionary nature of conventional innovation where big firms 'produce innovations that are associated with inequality', and that have little connection to low-income populations ([11], note 9 at 1), [58].

Indigenous innovation is rooted in the diverse and distinct cultures of Indigenous peoples' and tied to their long inhabitation in a particular place [59]. Indigenous innovation entails '...cultural autonomy, remembrance and retrieval, self-determination, and community-based values linked with the maintenance, preservation, restoration and revitalisation of indigenous knowledge systems that merge episteme with place and cultural practice.' Each of these aspects are 'continually articulated, debated, redefined, and expanded both within and outside of indigenous communities' ([59], at 4). Indigenous innovation develops in response to threats engendered by ecological and cultural challenges ([59], at 5), especially at the 'level of systems maintenance, where the systems being maintained are interlocking ecological systems and sub-systems' ([35], note 52 at 22).

However, TK holders' innovation marks a conceptual departure from the various domains of innovation, highlighted above, in a number of ways. It departs from inclusive innovation, in the sense that, the latter does not specify the 'marginalised' groups that it is concerned with. Indeed, the target group within inclusive innovation, tends to vary in different contexts ([58], note 88 at 4). TK holders' innovation focuses on TK holders. Local innovation differs from TK holders' innovation in that, with the former, the innovation may not have the necessary linkage to TK, culture, tradition or heritage of the innovators. Moreover, there is also no necessary link between the innovator and the relevant resources (plants and animals) in a cosmological sense. Further, local innovation connotes only context-specific and internal innovation, and is thus conceptually narrower than TK innovation ([52], note 79 at 1, 3). Hence, TK innovation can be described as local, but local innovation may not necessarily be TK innovation. There are relatively more overlaps between TK and Indigenous innovation than with the other types of innovation. While TK innovation is generally informed by TK, Indigenous innovation is underpinned by Indigenous knowledge (IK). TK is the 'totality of all knowledge and practices' used in the management of socio-economic and ecological facets of life while IK is the local knowledge unique to a particular culture and society that identifies itself as Indigenous ([9], note 7 at 3), [60, 61]. Nonetheless, TK and IK may also overlap depending on the political context and experiences of the claimants to the knowledge. For instance, the Indigenous people of North America, may describe IK the same way as TK, but their recognition in international law as Indigenous People, has a jurisprudential connotation that ties them to the use of IK, even though they may not support any suggestion that IK is not TK. Thus, TK holders' innovation is broader, and may encompass indigenous innovation. However, there is a convergence between Indigenous and TK innovation in that both are 'place-based' and 'cosmologically linked to land' in the sense that there is a special relationship between the innovators and a place ([35], note 52 at 2).

However, and for a long time, research and metrics on innovation has focused on innovation within large firms, to the extent that innovation (especially product innovation) is more often equated with R&D ([35], note 52 at 3), ([42], note 61 at 53-55), ([52], note 79), [62] expenditures than on informal means such as 'learning-by-doing,' 'learning-by-using,' 'learning on the job,' self-training and apprenticeships ([29], note 43 at 3-4), ([35], note 52 at 18), [63]. Moreover, conventional innovation metrics value the standardisation of innovation through either IP standards or levels of educational enrolment or attainment, hence inappropriate in investigating the nature, type and extent of TK holders' innovation ([42], note 61 at 55), ([29], note 43 at 21); which could be uncodified and transmitted transgenerationally ([35], note 52 at 18). Further, R&D is equated more or less with product innovation-intensive technological breakthroughs or, in IP circles, patentable inventions ([42], note 61 at 54), making it insufficient in the context of TK holders' innovations that are place-based, cumulative (limited newness), collectively developed and result from interactions with nature, and not R&D ([63], note 98 at 1599).

Thus, there is lack of comprehensive research outlining a coherent theoretical and practical account of TK innovation. Indeed, Rizk *et al* rightfully opine that TK is not included within the broader definition, and understanding of knowledge and innovation ([5], note 4 at 290), ([12], note 9 at 3-4), ([29], note 43 at 8), ([36], note 53), ([37], note 53). Consequently, there is a lack of research linking TK holders' institutions and innovation in Africa, more so in the context of the SDGs.

4.3 TK holders' institutions and building of strong institutions

As mentioned earlier, the popularity, legitimacy and resilience of TK holders' institutions means that they still play crucial roles in society. TK holders rely on these institutions in natural resources governance, conflict resolution, in maintenance of law and order, and even politics, as is illustrated in the case studies. This means that they can perform important roles in building and strengthening formal institutions, especially where the latter are weak or non-existent.

Social capital helps TK holders build important linkages, within and beyond the community, including with public and private institutions, which help in strengthening institutions ([33], note 50 at 37), ([34], note 52 at 10). The ability of TK holders' institutions to generate innovation, provides knowledge and capacity for implementing policy initiatives, and 'fill in the void created by the limited penetration of national institutions' especially 'in the presence of weak state capacity' [64]. For instance, with the institutional crisis bedevilling IP institutions in spurring and promoting TK holders' innovation among communities ([45], note 65 at 6), collaborations between TK holders' and IP institutions can enrich the latter, and address the inadequacy, deficiency and unsuitability of the IP regime in protecting TK. Such collaborations, can break the barrier to scaling up TK holders' innovative activity, for instance, if communities can have some 'exclusive rights' over their innovations, they might develop their businesses beyond a certain stage, and possibly be incentivised to invest in machines or human capital ([28], note 43 at 255). This is so because, the dynamics of innovation benefits from a system in which all actors (including TK holders and their institutions) in the innovation paradigm work together in a collaborative manner. Such collaborations enhance good governance, inclusivity in innovation and the building of strong institutions from below, as communities participate in the development dialogue.

Moreover, TK holders' institutions are able to address the gender gap and institutional barriers to innovation within the IP regime. For instance, in a study of Zulu women bead-workers, Desmond Oriakhogba demonstrates that through social entrepreneurship and inclusive innovation, rural women crafters are 'getting around the challenges within the IP regimes by developing a community which fosters inclusion, collaboration, knowledge-sharing and continuous learning among themselves' [65]. This way, the women are 'constantly improving and harnessing their indigenous knowledge and empowering themselves to be able to address their personal and shared social challenges of poverty, inadequate health care, housing, access to education for their children, among others' ([65], at 145-172).

4.4 TK holders' institutions and transformative entrepreneurship

UNCTAD identifies the institutional framework, as one of the priority areas in devising an entrepreneurship policy in developing countries [66]. The institutional framework has a strong impact on the type of entrepreneurship that arises, and its broader societal impact, including its contribution to structural transformation [67].

TK holders' institutions contain data that has a decisive impact on the prevalence, type and nature of entrepreneurial activities [68] that TK holders can engage in. The data also assists in determining if, how, and under what conditions community members can access available resources such as knowledge to generate output, skills, innovation, labour, finance etc. [68, 69].

Social capital enables TK holders access vital contacts, resources (markets, credit, and diverse domains of knowledge) and information by linking them to other social and economic agents, within the community and beyond, whose capabilities could boost entrepreneurship ([2], note 2 at 20), ([34], note 52 at 10), ([45], note 65 at 3), ([33], note 50 at 37). Conversely, the new actors (entrepreneurs) provide the necessary resources needed in the innovation process such as tools, production equipment, access to seed capital and grant funds for innovation development [33]. Thus, while spurring innovation, TK holders' institutions also enhance and promote their entrepreneurial spirit ([51], note 76 at 9), ([67], note 111 at 11), [70].

Successful entrepreneurship is also seen as 'a cooperative endeavour, mediated by social networks' rather than 'a purely individualistic and competitive' effort [70]. Consequently, the environment within which entrepreneurship takes place impacts its nature and success. Rutert and Traynor show in their research that TK holders are social entrepreneurs ([54], note 82 at 5), ([67], note 111 at 9) who generate process innovations, for example, in 'networking, collaboration, group formation, and organisational governance and management practices' ([54], note 82 at 4). These activities are entrepreneurial, irrespective of their economic outputs, as they not only produce 'tangible, alienable (economic) values' but also develop 'inalienable (social) values and (inter)actions' ([54], at 5). Likewise, Oriakhogba's study shows how rural Zulu women bead workers, are addressing personal and shared social challenges of poverty, inadequate health care, housing, access to education for their children, among others, through social entrepreneurship and inclusive innovation ([65], note 108 at 145-172). Thus, TK holders engage in entrepreneurship to meet local needs due to gaps left by a State, which is no longer supplying the much-needed products and services [71, 72].

TK holders' institutions, also hold great promise in driving transformational entrepreneurship among TK holders, since transformational entrepreneurship foresees the possibility of transformational contribution by non-firms, that is, organisations such as cooperatives, non-governmental organisations and public institutions [73]. Be that as it may, existing literature has not critically examined the role of TK holders' and their institutions in promoting entrepreneurship yet they hold vital data that can be tapped to spur entrepreneurship for community benefit.

4.5 TK holders' institutions, data and data governance

TK holders' institutions are data repositories explaining why they are able to generate innovations, and contribute towards the strengthening of other institutions. Through the institutions, vital data is collected, shared, analysed and applied to provide expertise, monitor, plan, and manage disasters such as drought, famine, disease or bad omen to the community ([18], note 16 at 11). For instance, the Afar pastoralists in Ethiopia are able to predict weather and climate through the observation of stars, winds, livestock, insects, birds, trees and other wildlife [74].

While data is defined as 'factual information that has been collected together for reference or analysis, or numerical information represented in a form suitable for computer processing' ([6], note 4 at 18) in the context of Indigenous peoples, the term refers to 'information or knowledge, in any format or medium, which is about and may affect Indigenous peoples both collectively and individually' [75]. Data is a critical tool for advancing and attaining the cardinal objectives and development aspirations of Indigenous Peoples [76] including realising the right to self-determination. However, data is intimately linked to the sovereignty and self-determination of all nations ([76], at 4) hence the term data sovereignty, which refers to the right of States in relation to other States or entities to govern the collection, ownership, access and use of data within its jurisdiction [76, 77]. Consequently, the concept of data sovereignty allows States to control and own data belonging to TK holders (some of whom are Indigenous peoples).

Due to contestation over the sovereignty of Indigenous peoples and some of their rights in specific national contexts, they have had a troubled relationship since colonial times regarding how data concerning them is generated, accessed, shared, applied and owned by the State ([47], note 128 at 4). This is in spite of the fact that their ability to realise their rights to self-determination and leverage their development aspirations is anchored, to a large degree, on the issue of data sovereignty ([47], at 10).

While the conventional conceptions of the term data are broad, this study conceptualises the term data narrowly, by focusing on the TK that is generated, maintained, controlled, protected and developed by a community, and that is essential to their survival and livelihoods. Such TK (data), is developed within, and through TK institutions.

The data produced by TK holders provides 'information, guidance, help and support and gain most from developing social capital' ([31], note 126). In the context of Indigenous peoples, 'authentic data drives policy formulation, decision making and mapping of development aspirations, problem solving and other calculations critical to Indigenous resurgence in a range of fields' ([47], note 128 at 5). Moreover, data produces ways of doing which are unique to a specific place ([52], note 79 at 4); and is responsible for 'the effective and sustainable expansion of the capabilities and opportunities of the poor' [12, 78]. This is because it is accessible and applicable, and communities are able to effectively build on it to create innovative processes ([34], note 52 at 10). In a collaborative context, TK can 'empower other types of knowledge and innovation,' ([29], note 43 at 31) explaining why development activities that work with and within TK and traditional institutions have several advantages over projects that operate outside them ([34], note 52 at 10). Indeed, development agencies including the World Bank recognise the importance of integrating TK into development and poverty eradication ventures ([78], note 136 at 3) yet there is little research about the role of TK in innovation policies and ISs ([57], note 87 at 90).

The social networks created by TK holders around their innovations do enhance their capacities to create, use and disseminate TK ([34], note 52 at 1). As noted earlier, such networks interface with external networks, thus giving insights into how TK holders' innovation can be influenced by, or interact with, scientific (secondary) innovation specifically, and formal systems at large. While this interaction can result in the revitalisation of TK, it might occasion the conversion of TK into commodities that are controlled by new elites, due to power imbalances ([34], note 52 at 1). This is so because some of the efforts at revitalisation of TK, such as documentation, may among other things, alienate the relevant TK from the "protocols and epistemologies in which they were previously embedded" ([34], note 52 at 1). In addition, engagement with external actors may invoke concerns regarding what kind of TK should be disclosed in local innovation networks, and what should not. Moreover, engagement with external entities, primarily science-based innovation firms, tends to fill the void left by insufficient government investment in TK, only in instances where they become entitled to the appropriation of TK through the IP system [79]. This justifies an exploration of TK holders' institutions, and the roles they can perhaps play, in defining what constitutes TK holders' data, and appropriate ways of securing that data.

5. Findings and analysis

5.1 TK holders' institutions: nature and existence

In the case studies, there is evidence of existence of TK holders' institutions, in the form of customary laws, customs, traditions, family secrets, oral agreements, sharing mechanisms, community sanctions, trust, councils of elders, social capital and individuals holding specialised TK.

TK holders' institutions are grassroots decision-making units through which diverse social problems are identified and solutions provided at the local level. For instance, among the Mijikenda, the *kaya* elders seem to perform most of the functions listed by Mowo *et al*. In the Mbeere case study, the main institution in charge of traditional pottery are elderly women [80], who do not have many other roles in the community like the *kaya* elders.

As mentioned earlier, TK holders' institutions are governance frameworks that provide answers to contemporary problems faced by TK holders, as evidenced by the work of *kaya* elders in conservation. As data repositories, they play a central role in the creation, diffusion and application of innovation; while the innovation they generate continues to replenish and strengthen them. This also explains why those institutions can boost and contribute to peace, justice and the building of strong institutions.

Unlike conventional IP institutions, TK holders' institutions take a more inclusive and pragmatic approach to gender, as demonstrated by the prominent role played by elderly Mbeere women in conducting traditional pottery and transmitting those skills to young women. Studies have shown that the IP system does promote gender bias against women innovators and creators ([10], note 8 at 551-584) demonstrating its inappropriateness in promoting and protecting innovative activities by women. Therefore, TK holders' institutions are able to accommodate the participation of women, and even men depending on a given context as aspects of their gender inclusivity in innovation. Further, they thus produce varied innovations that may deal with a wide range of social problems, such as environmental degradation, and poverty that may affect different segments of society.

5.2 Roles of TK holders' institutions in promoting innovation

TK holders' institutions have a role in advancing innovation. Those institutions (social capital/networks) provide what De Beer *et al* describe as a 'local innovation system' ([42], note 61 at 60). They are the space that supports learning, knowledge production and utilisation; innovation promotion and exchange; and flow of knowledge and innovation ([34], note 52 at 1). In the Mbeere case study, senior women transmit intergenerationally pottery skills and practices to young women, either through apprenticeships or experiential learning [80]. Similarly, among the *kaya* elders, TK can be passed through divine intervention, for instance, where prophets get information on different calamities, diseases and outbreaks, and pass the same to elders [22]. The respective innovations have thus survived courtesy of the institutional dynamics that allow the flow and transmission of innovation intergenerationally.

TK holders' institutions allow communities to enhance their innovative capacity, and expand their institutional networks, at the local level and beyond. This increases their innovation output, as they access information and learn new techniques of production. The General Coordinator of ABN explained that in their work they 'encourage the sharing of seeds within and outside communities to encourage diversity' [81]. The *kaya* elders have had a collaboration with UNESCO, where the latter supported the formation of the Mijikenda Council of Elders for all the nine sub-communities, and gave funding to hire forest guards [22]. Moreover, UNESCO has donated funds that were used to give awards to *kayas* that are doing well in conservation thus incentivising elders and enhance competitiveness in conservation [22]. Thus, strengthening TK holders' institutions, would correspondingly enable communities to collaborate effectively with relevant actors, and help advance their innovation activities.

TK holders' innovations are mainly geared towards meeting some social goals (drawing parallels with social innovation), and not necessarily profit making. One respondent indicated that 'the driving force for TK holders is not economic but revitalization of knowledge and practices' [81]. Among the Mbeere people, pottery was not done for sale, although nowadays this has changed [80]. Additionally, the goals and expression of TK holders' innovations, at times, have less to do with products, and everything to do with services to society. The innovations tend to take the form of 'services to the land' with huge public benefits in terms of biodiversity, and environmental and climate values, which are not easily convertible into income streams ([35], note 52 at 24). The *kaya* elders have through long interaction with their environment, developed innovative practices and systems for regulating access to the forests, medicinal plants, sacred *kaya* areas, rare species, traditional knowledge and agricultural activities [21]. Moreover, the pottery activities of the Mbeere women contributes to firewood conservation, as the traditional pots retain more heat than normal cooking pots [82]. According to the General Coordinator of African Biodiversity Network (ABN),

> *"The greatest contribution of communities to SDGs mostly is in climate change, environment and water. The revival of seeds, biodiversity and ecosystems contributes to SDGs because we work in a holistic manner. This work contributes to adaptation and improved nutritional levels amongst the communities." [81].*

Through bridging social capital, TK holders' institutions act as special vehicles that promote the commercialisation and efficient diffusion of innovation in society ([51], note 76 at 9). For instance, the *kaya* elders have collaborated with TICAH, a CSO, in efforts towards documenting and commercialising their traditional medicine. The *kaya* elders provided knowledge on plants with various healing properties, while TICAH offered training on various ways of preparing drugs for purposes of commercialisation and wider reach of the drugs. The elders indicated that the collaboration was successful, and it helped improve the relationship between the youth and elders [22]. They have also collaborated with NMK in preserving their TK, traditions and cultures, and with the county government of Kilifi in having forest guards to protect the forests [82].

Whereas through collaborations, TK can empower other types of knowledge and innovation ([29], note 43 at 31), as mentioned earlier, collaborations aimed at commercialisation, may occasion the loss of TK and innovation, especially if they are not carried out through TK holders' institutions. For instance, efforts by the government and some non-governmental organisations to introduce the throwing wheel (a modern technique of making pots instead of hand pottery) among the pottery communities to make the process more efficient and less labour intensive, was rejected by potters so as to preserve the sanctity of cultural and communal processes of knowledge production [83]. Moreover, they may have rejected mechanised production as it is likely to weaken traditional institutions due to less reliance on TK and related practices. Further, they could have been motivated by market demands, since hand-made and home-made crafts and cuisines respectively, tend to attract higher value than mechanised and mass produced/commercial counterparts of the same crafts. To preserve the sanctity of cultural and traditional processes of production, from adulteration and destruction, there is need to strengthen TK holders' institutions.

Further, TK holders' institutions can also facilitate the adaptation of new innovation and technologies to local needs and conditions by, *inter alia,* improving access to, and management of natural resources, sharing experiences, facilitating access to inputs and outputs, offering training, improving the availability of information, strengthening bargaining power with intermediaries and participating in public research and extension ([45], note 65 at 4), ([51], note 76 at 10). For instance, whereas the pottery practices and skills of the Mbeere have been transmitted intergenerationally [80], there are new designs and/or shapes that the community is developing. A good example is vessels designed for planting flowers, which have perforated bases, to serve as flower vases. Such shapes and designs have not been archaeologically discovered ([27], note 35 at 62) meaning they are new additions to the design repertoire.

The fact that TK holders' institutions take a pragmatic approach to gender suggests that they engender inclusivity in innovation processes by enabling women, men and other social groups in a community to participate and benefit from innovations ([11], note 9 at 5). The Mbeere case study shows that TK holders' innovation is gendered. Traditional pottery is a preserve of women since time immemorial, and men only offer ancillary support, such as transportation of large clay bags to the potting sites, or of finished pots to the market [11]. This contrasts with the Mijikenda, where the *kaya* elders are mostly men. Thus, TK holders' innovation and processes have a pragmatic approach to gender, and offer women opportunities to innovate, participate in, and benefit from innovation processes ([12], note 9 at 7). Strengthening TK holders' institutions will allow both men and women to participate in and benefit from innovation, and diversify the innovation and innovation processes, creating more opportunities for the community to better their livelihoods.

5.3 Roles of TK holders' institutions in the building and strengthening of other institutions

The popularity, resilience and legitimacy of TK holders' institutions suggests that there is need to interrogate how they can be harnessed to promote the building of strong institutions in view of failure by most African governments to provide critical goods and services to communities.

As custodial institutions, TK holders' institutions are being used in the case studies to regulate access to and use of natural resources (including associated TK). Among the Mijikenda, the governance of the *kaya* forests is through customary rules that are enforced by elders using traditional sanctions to censor misuse of resources [84]. The *kaya* elders 'control access to resources such as medicinal plants, sacred *kaya* areas, and rare species; traditional knowledge and agricultural activities' and 'are the ones who allocate those resources to clans and individuals' [21]. Indeed, the very existence of the *kaya* forests is attributed to the work of elders in conservation, and not gazettement as a forest reserve, national monument or listing as a world heritage site [84]. The demarcation, surveying, and mapping of territories; gazettement as national monuments and listing of the *kaya* forests, as World Heritage Sites is done with the assistance of elders and other community members [84]. The role of the *kaya* elders in environmental conservation is thus useful in realising other SDGs such as energy (SDG-7), food (SDG-2), water (SDG-6) and climate action (SDG-13), and ultimately in strengthening formal institutions dealing with these SDGs.

Moreover, social capital contributes to the strengthening of both the TK holders' and formal institutions involved in the collaboration. As communities begin to work together, bonding social capital is strengthened within the group, particularly in terms of trust between members, the development of group norms, roles, and processes, and the development of a sense of 'can-do spirit' within the group which contributes to a growing sense of collective efficacy [17]. This explains why TK holders' institutions promote cultural unity and identity. For instance, the *kaya* elders and forests, are seen as a significant unifying factor for the Mijikenda people. The *kaya* forests are the 'cultural and traditional home' of the Mijikenda that 'serves to remind them and future generations of how they migrated from Shungwaya to that place' [85].

Bridging social capital within TK holders' institutions enhances collaborations between those institutions and other institutions. Government agencies and civil society actors are relying on these institutions in their work of protecting and preserving TK. Among the Mijikenda, there are on and off collaborations between elders and NMK in preserving traditions and cultures [86]. For instance, *kaya* elders participated in the preparation of the 2014–2018 Mijikenda Kaya Forest Management Plan prepared by NMK. In conservation, herbalists from *kaya* Kauma have collaborated with the Gede Kenya Forest Research Institute (KEFRI) regional headquarters to get technical advice on research programs that can improve the mangrove forest medicinal value. Moreover, they contributed in the preparation of the National Mangrove Management Plan being developed by the Kenya Marine and Fisheries Research Institute (KEMFRI). One respondent lamented how the engagement with formal state institutions has been disrespectful and contemptuous of TK institutions, thus hampering their effective incorporation in governance [86]. In Mbeere, while the potters are usually invited to schools to teach students how to make pots, the respondents indicated that there are no CSOs that supports their pottery practices [80].

As mentioned earlier, collaborations between TK holders' institutions and the IP frameworks can enrich the IP regime and address the inadequacy, deficiency and unsuitability of the IP regime in protecting TK. Effectively, they can mediate interactions between the IP system and TK holders, and thus tame the misappropriation and loss of TK and genetic resources. For instance, TK holders' institutions can be used in granting prior informed consent (PIC) and in developing bio-cultural protocols to govern access to TK [87]. Additionally, having PIC and disclosure of origin as a criterion for patentability, would benefit TK holders since their institutions could be involved in the decision-making processes and institutions under the IP regime and *vice versa*. This collaboration can bridge the TK protection gap as TK holders can withhold their PIC so as to safeguard their rights, while the grant of IP rights over TK could also be withheld by relevant authorities, if there is non-disclosure of origin or proof of PIC is missing. This way the TK holders' institutions will contribute to the strengthening of IP institutions.

Moreover, the participation of women in TK holders' innovation (as is the case with the Mbeere potters) can help address institutional barriers to innovation created by the IP regimes. This way, TK holders' institutions can strengthen the IP policies, laws and institutions by making them gender sensitive by including women in decision-making processes, as key agents of innovation.

Similarly, TK holders' institutions are used in determining political leadership and maintenance of law and order. The *kaya* elders were described 'as a social-political epicentre of the Mijikenda people that is resorted to even by local politicians for blessings before venturing into politics' [21]. It is commonplace for those vying for political positions to seek the endorsement of the *kaya* elders. Clearly, they can play a role in strengthening political institutions, and in holding elected leaders to account.

As customary governance systems, TK holders' institutions are being used in conflict resolution among the Mijikenda. The *kaya* elders are the first port of call wherever there are disputes (including land, family and political) in the community [87]. They therefore contribute to enhanced access to justice, and strengthen institutions of justice.

5.4 Roles of TK holders' institutions in driving transformative entrepreneurship

Due to their role in driving innovation, TK holders' institutions provide a conducive environment for entrepreneurship, as they enhance the entrepreneurial capabilities and mind-set in the community.

As mentioned earlier, TK holders are 'not-for-profit entrepreneurs' as they mainly pursue social and collective goals. For instance, the conservation work of the *kaya* elders. However, that is not to say that they cannot derive economic benefits out of their entrepreneurial work. Some communities have traded, and are ready to convert some of their TK products and entrepreneurial activities into income generating ventures to improve their livelihoods. Among the *kaya* elders there are income generating activities such as establishment of tree nurseries, poultry farming and so on, aimed at reducing community dependency on natural resources for livelihood [86]. In *kaya* Kauma, there are plans to start levying students, researchers and tourists who may want to pay a visit to the permitted parts of the *kaya*. Additionally, there is a plan to register traditional songs and dances of the Kauma and provide entertainment services during government events and other communal gatherings [87].

In Mbeere, whereas pottery plays cultural functions in the community, it is a source of livelihood to the potter. Thus, nowadays pottery is a complementary source of income to the women who sell their pots on market days especially in Ishiara town. Wangari explains that the shift towards commercialisation of pottery, is occasioned by the demand for pottery in neighbouring regions such as Nyeri, Mururi, Kerugoya, Murang'a and Meru where pottery making does not take place ([27], note 35 at 78). The Mbeere potters explained that they are not paid *per se* for training school children traditional pottery, but only get refund for transport expenses, costs for transporting soil and a small token for the days spent training [80]. This allows the women to generate some income, and gives them an incentive to continually look for new training opportunities, and create new networks and social relations, thus engender entrepreneurship. Likewise, among the Mijikenda, plans to introduce income-generating activities by a CSO, Careway-Trust such as putting up tree nurseries, inventory of a craft industry, window curtains or manufacturing workshop are meant to reduce community dependence on the *kaya* forests for livelihoods/subsistence needs [88]. Therefore, strengthening TK holders' institutions, will not only advance innovation, but will help safeguard their survival and livelihoods, which are met through their innovative activities.

The intangible capacities within TK holders' institutions continue to enhance and promote TK holders' entrepreneurial spirit. For instance, the Mbeere women indicated that the people they sell their pots to are their ambassadors, as they market their pots and activities to other people and organisations [80].

There are other entrepreneurship initiatives around the conservation work of the Mijikenda people. For example, a community-based organisation, Care Way-Trust has come up with different thematic areas to promote entrepreneurship. One scheme called '*tubadilike* scheme' seeks to introduce bee keeping around *kaya* forests, educating the wider community on terrestrial tree nurseries in their homes and starting grafting of citrus trees as income generating activities [89]. The '*mtoto asome*' seeks to create awareness among the youth on the importance of environmental conservation by teaching them techniques on tree planting for income generation.

5.5 Roles of TK holders' institutions in data governance

TK holders' institutions are data repositories and data governance structures holding data on community affairs such as knowledge, beliefs, values, 'regularised practices', customary rules, norms and practices. In the case studies, most data is gathered, stored and transmitted intergenerationally through TK holders' institutions. Among the Mijikenda, traditional ceremonies, rituals, prayers, and legends play a critical role in storage and sharing of information and knowledge [22]. A respondent stated that, 'cultural rituals for example the rites of passage in most communities provide a system of transmitting and guarding TK' since 'as one goes through the rites of passage, there is knowledge that is passed on to initiates' [81]. Some reports document how legends are used to pass on rules against cutting trees, fishing, hunting or cultivating in the sacred sites, among the Meru people of Kenya [90]. Moreover, there are legends about the ability of sacred sites to self-protect themselves 'from destruction by reacting and attacking any person who interfered with them by venturing into or doing anything forbidden at the sites' [90]. Similarly, the *kaya* elders explained that at times they 'rely on prophets who get information through divine intervention on how to deal with different calamities, diseases and outbreaks. That information is then given to elders' [22]. Data governance among the Mijikenda has a divine aspect in the sense that "once an elder die (chairman), elders keep his record/memory in a *kigango*, which represents the dead *kaya* elder and continues to 'speak' on his behalf." [90]. The elders explained that most of these *vigango* were stolen and taken to museums abroad, although there are efforts to repatriate them.

As data governance structures, they are the forum through which community decisions and norms are made [91] including regulating who can access, use, add data and have control of communal resources [92]. Among the Mijikenda, 'the *kambi* controls access to resources such as medicinal plants, sacred *kaya* areas, and rare species; traditional knowledge and agricultural activities' and 'are the ones who allocate those resources to clans and individuals' [21]. Access, use and sharing of data within the community is mediated by core principles like trust, honour, and integrity ([92], note 233 at 12). While common knowledge may easily be accessible, secret and sacred TK might not be accessible. This has significant implications since it means that secret and sacred TK might not be a proper subject of innovation collaborations and entrepreneurship because for local innovation to thrive, it is essential that the infrastructure and networks relating to it is disclosed to actors outside the circle of local innovators themselves.

The role of traditional institutions in TK governance includes: the identification of TK; ascertainment of beneficiaries; definition of custodianship; the nature of community custodianship over TK; the rights and responsibilities associated with custody, access rights, protection of customary use, means of dissemination and preservation of knowledge; and the customary mode of defining modalities of PIC, benefit sharing mechanisms, dispute settlement, and sanctions for infringement of customary law ([69, 93], note 113), [93].

In addition, the TK held by communities is 'a key element of the social capital of the poor and constitutes their main asset in their efforts to gain control of their own lives' ([78], note 136 at 1). Moreover, TK is 'the basis for decisions pertaining to food security, human and animal health, education, natural resources management, and other vital activities' ([78], note 136 at 1). Among the Mbeere, for example, pot making is done during the dry season (August–October) because they can easily get dry grass and wood to harden the pots [80]. Further, reliance on TK holders' institutions in conflict resolution reveals that they hold vital information that aids in mediation of disputes with high degrees of societal and ecological complexity, as demonstrated by the work of *kaya* elders [21].

Evidently, the above discussion shows that TK holders' institutions are pivotal in designing a strong regime for TK holders' data sovereignty ([47], note 128 at 12-14). Those institutions are better placed than formal state institutions in defining what constitutes data, outlining appropriate ways of securing the data, and governing control, use or reuse of their data by third parties, even where such data is gathered in the context of research studies. Indeed, one cannot conduct research among communities, such as the Mijikenda, without an ethical clearance and permission. Thereafter, the *kaya* elders determine the data and areas (within a *kaya*) that a researcher can access. Further, reliance on TK holders' institutions in developing community bio-cultural protocols and granting PIC [94], strongly suggests that it is indeed possible to develop a collaborative framework where those institutions can be legally mandated with TK holders' data governance.

5.6 Challenges bedevilling TK holders' institutions

In spite of the existence of TK holders' institutions in both case studies, their vitality and influence are waning due to a multiplicity of factors. These include, leadership wrangles among elders, each claiming to be the legitimate elders; cultural erosion; loss of Indigenous territories due to developmental projects; and the influence of modern education and religions, which have contributed to the loss of traditional beliefs and values. For instance, among the Mbeere, young women and girls see pottery as 'foolishness and shameful' and have no interest in the art and practice. One respondent, who has practiced pottery for over 50 years, indicated that 'my daughter is almost 40 years but does not want to learn the practice' [80]. In the Mijikenda community, a negative perception towards elders has occasioned numerous attacks and killings of elders. One elder observed that, 'We will die with our knowledge, we are seen as witches. We are being killed because of white hair. We are not seen as good people' [95]. However, the elders indicated that they continue to conduct prayers, cultural rituals and other traditions to continually replenish and revitalise their TK and cultural expressions so that they are not lost [96]. Similarly, urbanisation has contributed to the low demand for pottery because many people in towns have resorted to the use of gas and electric cookers as compared to the pots that are commonly used on *jikos* and hearthstones ([27], note 35 at 86). However, and inasmuch as traditional pots are commonly used in cooking with firewood (in which case they are more energy efficient than ordinary aluminium pots), they can also be used with gas and electric cookers (which are more energy friendly than firewood) thus promoting conservation.

Most TK holders are living in poverty, and are experiencing capacity, financial, educational, skills, information, and infrastructure constraints to innovate on a large scale. Likewise, these constraints are also hindering entrepreneurship among TK holders and beyond due to lack of essential skills for business organisation such as 'writing, reading, bookkeeping, project management, and even (potentially) fluency in the English language' ([54], cit note 82 at 7). The Mbeere potters face difficulties when transporting pots to distant markets due to their bulkiness and fragility, and lack expertise for mass production of pots to meet rising demands for pots, and get more income to meet survival and livelihood needs [82]. However, earlier studies show that the potters had shunned mechanised forms of production ([83], cit note 165). To scale up and commercialise (if permissible by the holders) some of their innovations, TK holders can utilise their institutions to enter into collaborations with other players to develop (according to their terms) and diffuse them. Nonetheless, there is need for caution in embracing modern systems of production, as they may erode the innovative capacity of TK holders and their institutions. Moreover, and as observed earlier, there are people who still prefer hand-made crafts as opposed to machine-made ones, for cultural, aesthetic, and functional reasons, which are factors that create demand for hand-made products. Hence those collaborations must acknowledge the value and potential for TK to empower other forms of knowledge and innovation.

The respondents lamented lack of support from government and CSOs. The author observed the lack of programs from CSOs or government to support and promote the pottery practices of the Mbeere. Unless there are concerted efforts to support the Mbeere women, the traditional pottery practices are likely to become extinct. As opined earlier, through their institutions, TK holders can increase their innovation output, learn new techniques of production, but also document their pottery knowledge and techniques, so that they can remain sustainable.

Similarly, the *kaya* elders observed that there is tension between them and chiefs and sub-chiefs, and in most cases the latter do not recognise or engage them in community affairs [22]. Finally, the *kaya* elders decried the fact that although they 'bless' or endorse secular or political actors, those leaders end up undermining them once they get power [83].

6. Conclusions

The study sought to examine the role of TK holders' institutions in the realisation of SDG-9 (the study focused on innovation) and SDG-16 (study focused on the building of strong institutions) using the Mijikenda and Mbeere communities in Kenya. The study finds the existence of TK holders' institutions in the case studies. They have been resilient and are legitimate explaining their continued use in natural resources governance, conflict resolution and even in politics. Importantly, the findings show that the institutions have a role in driving innovation, building strong institutions, engendering entrepreneurship and as data governance structures.

Regarding innovation, the study has shown that TK holders' institutions are instrumental in enhancing the innovation capacity of TK holders by creating the space that supports learning, creation and utilisation of innovation; promotion of innovation; and the flow and exchange of innovation. The institutions also increase the innovation output of TK holders, by enabling the latter access information and learn new techniques of production. Additionally, the institutions allow TK holders to expand institutional networks, at the local level and beyond, thus accessing resources to advance their innovation. Through those networks, TK holders' institutions promote the commercialisation and efficient diffusion of innovation in society; and facilitate the adaptation of new innovation and technologies to local needs and conditions. Further, and due to their pragmatic approach to gender, they engender inclusivity in innovation processes by enabling women, men and other social groups in a community to participate and benefit from innovations. Lastly, TK holders' institutions are better placed in protecting TK holders' innovation in view of the challenges they encounter in using the IP systems. However, and whereas TK holders, are likely to benefit from collaborations with formal institutions like the IP framework in promoting their innovations and transformational entrepreneurship, those collaborations ought to be built through strong institutions that are dynamic, flexible, locally legitimate and responsive to social, political and environmental changes. Reliance on stronger TK holders' institutions can help stop the disenfranchising outcomes while interacting with external networks, and uphold communities' self-determining rights.

In the building of strong institutions as desired by SDG-16, the study has shown that TK holders' institutions continue to enjoy popular legitimacy, and play an essential role in conflict resolution, natural resources governance, in determining political leadership and maintenance of law and order, especially in the Mijikenda case study. As such, they can be used collaboratively with formal institutions like the justice system, natural resources governance institutions, and the IP system, to build strong and inclusive governance frameworks. From the case studies, it is evident that unlike the IP regime, TK holders' institutions have an inclusive and pragmatic approach to gender (thus promoting attainment of SDG-16 by being inclusive), offering both men and women opportunities to participate in, and benefit from innovation processes (essentially meeting SDG-9 by encouraging inclusivity in innovation). The study shows that the role of TK holders' institutions in the attainment of SDG-9 and 16 contributes positively in the realisation of other SDGs also. Some of the innovative activities that TK holders are engaged in, such as conservation of the environment, and making of pots that are energy efficient, can contribute to advancing other SDGs such as energy (SDG-7), climate action (SDG-13), food (SDG-2), life on land (SDG-15) and water (SDG-6).

Due to their role in driving innovation, TK holders' institutions provide a conducive environment for entrepreneurship, as they enhance the entrepreneurial capabilities and mind-set in the community. They also determine the prevalence, type and nature of entrepreneurial activities that TK holders engage in. through bridging social capital, TK holders are able to link up with other social and economic agents, and thus access vital resources, infrastructure, skills and knowledge within the community and beyond, which boost entrepreneurship.

Lastly, the study has shown that TK holders' institutions are pivotal in designing a strong regime for TK holders' data sovereignty, as they are data repositories and data governance frameworks. The data they hold underlies their capacity to innovate; strengthens institutions; manage, monitor and mitigate risks; and has impact on prevalence, type and nature of entrepreneurial activities that they can engage in. As data governance frameworks, they hold the promise in the realisation of the developmental needs and aspirations of TK holders.

Author details

Francis Kariuki
Strathmore University Law School, Nairobi, Kenya

*Address all correspondence to: kariukifrancis06@gmail.com

IntechOpen

© 2021 The Author(s). Licensee IntechOpen. This chapter is distributed under the terms of the Creative Commons Attribution License (http://creativecommons.org/licenses/by/3.0), which permits unrestricted use, distribution, and reproduction in any medium, provided the original work is properly cited.

References

[1] Paula Donnelly-Roark, Karim Ouedraogo, and Xiao Ye, 2001 'Can local institutions reduce poverty? Rural decentralization in Burkina Faso' *Policy Research Working Paper 2677*, Environmental and Social Development Unit, Africa region (2001) at 3.

[2] Jeremias Mowo, Zenebe Adimassu, Kenneth Masuki, Charles Lyamchai, Joseph Tanui & Delia Catacutan 'The Importance of Local Traditional Institutions in the Management of Natural Resources in the Highlands of Eastern Africa' *Working Paper No 134*, World Agroforestry Centre (2011) at 7-12.

[3] Different terms have been used to describe TK holders' institutions including indigenous, customary, traditional or informal.

[4] Sujai Shivakumar 'The Place of Indigenous Institutions in Constitutional Order' 14(1) (2003) *Constitutional Political Economy* at 10

[5] Elizabeth Watson 'Examining the Potential of Indigenous Institutions for Development' (2003) *Development and Change* at 287-309

[6] Shirin Elahi, Jeremy de Beer, Dick Kawooya, Chidi Oguamanam & Nagla Rizk, *Knowledge and Innovation in Africa: Scenarios for the Future* (Open AIR, 2013) at 126.

[7] Available at https://sdg-tracker.org/infrastructure-industrialization, accessed on 16/01/2020.

[8] Available at https://www.un.org/development/desa/disabilities/envision2030-goal16.html, accessed on 16/01/2020.

[9] See Mugabe John 'Intellectual Property Protection and Traditional Knowledge: An Exploration in International Policy Discourse' (2001) at 25.

[10] Ann Bartow 'Fair use and the fairer sex: Gender, feminism, and copyright law' (2006) 14(3) *Journal of Gender, Social Policy & the Law* at 551 – 584.

[11] Patti Petesch, Lone Badstue,Gordon Prain, Marlene Elias & Amare Tegbaru 'Entry points for enabling gender equality in agricultural and environmental innovation' GENNOVATE resources for scientists and research teams (2017) at 5.

[12] See Julio Berdegue 'Pro-poor innovation systems' Background Paper, IFAD (2005) at 7.

[13] SDG-15 requires the protection, restoration and promotion of sustainable use of ecosystems, forests, combat desertification and halt land and biodiversity degradation.

[14] SDG-13 *inter alia*, seeks to strengthen resilience and adaptive capacity to climate-related hazards and natural disasters; and improve education and awareness-rising and human and institutional capacity on climate change mitigation, adaptation, impact reduction and early warning.

[15] I obtained ethics clearance from the Strathmore University Institutional Ethics Review Committee (SU-IERC) which is one of the accredited institutions by the National Commission for Science, Technology and Innovation (NACOSTI) in Kenya to conduct ethics reviews of research protocols in the human and behavioral sciences.

[16] Paul Ongugo, Doris Mutta, Mohamed Pakia & Peter Munyi 'Protecting Traditional Health Knowledge in Kenya: The role of customary laws and practices' International Institute for Environment and Development (2012) at 4.

[17] James de V. Azzen & Jim Allen 'Shungwaya, the Mijikenda, and the Traditions' (1983) 16(3) *The International Journal of African Historical Studies*, 455-485 at 455.

[18] Celia Nyamweru 'Sacred Groves and Environmental Conservation' (1998) *The 1998 Frank P. Pistor Faculty Lecture*, 1-27 at 9.

[19] Celia Nyamweru 'Report on Socio-Cultural Research carried out in Kwale and Kilifi Districts of Kenyan' unpublished manuscript, at 12 (a copy in the researcher's file).

[20] Interview with an environmental scientist working with the CFCU at Kilifi on 05/11/2019. Some trees are sacred, and are believed to be the abode or shelter of ancestral spirits as well as the secret objects of the community and cannot be harvested.

[21] Interview with an environmental scientist working with the CFCU at Kilifi on 05/11/2019.

[22] A meeting with *kaya* elders at Kaloleni on 04/11/2019.

[23] Celia Nyamweru & Elias Kimaru 'The contribution of ecotourism to the conservation of natural sacred sites: A case study from coastal Kenya' (2008) 2(3) *JSRNC*, 327-350 at 328.

[24] For example, *kaya* Mudzimwiru, Mudzimuvya and Bomu-Fimboni; Fungo, Kambe, Kauma, Ribe, Kinondo and Jibana.

[25] Available at https://www.ticahealth.org/indigenous-knowledge-culture/indigenous-knowledge-culture/ accessed on 16/01/2020.

[26] Workshop with traditional potters in Ishiara held on 13/11/2019.

[27] Rosemary Wangari 'An ethnoarchaeological study of pottery in Evurore division, Mbeere North District, Embu county, Kenya' Master of Arts Thesis, Kenyatta University (2013) at 35.

[28] Jeremy de Beer & Sacha Wunsch-Vincent 'Appropriation and Intellectual Property in the Informal Economy' in Erica Kraemer-Mbula & Sacha Wunsch-Vincent (eds.) *The Informal Economy in Developing Nations-Hidden engine of innovation?* (Cambridge University Press, 2016) at 243

[29] See also Nagla Rizk, Ayah El Said, Nadine Weheba & Jeremy de Beer 'Towards an Alternative Assessment of Innovation in Africa' OpenAir, *Working Paper 10* (2018) at 40.

[30] Carolyn Logan 'The roots of resilience: Exploring popular support for African traditional authorities' (2013) 112(448) *African Affairs,* 353-376 at 358.

[31] Judith Kamoto, Graham Clarkson, Peter Dorward & Derek Shepherd 'Doing more harm than good? Community based natural resource management and the neglect of local institutions in policy development' (2013) 35 *Land Use Policy* at 293-301 at 293

[32] See also Heidi Wittmer, Felix Rauschmayer & Bernd Klauer 'How to select instruments for the resolution of environmental conflicts?' (2006) 23 *Land Use Policy*, 1-9 at 4.

[33] Moina Rauf 'Innovations and informal institutions: An institutionalist approach to the role of social capital for innovation' (2009) *Journal of Academic Research in Economics* at 34.

[34] Maria-Constanza Torri & Julie Laplante 'Enhancing innovation between scientific and indigenous knowledge: pioneer NGOs in India' 5(29) (2009) *Journal of ethnobiology and ethnomedicine* at 1.

[35] See Peter Drahos & Susy Frankel 'Indigenous peoples' innovation and intellectual property: The issues' in Peter Drahos & Susy Frankel (eds.) *Indigenous peoples' innovation: Intellectual Property Pathways to Development* (ANU Press, 2012) at 4.

[36] Frances Cleaver 'Moral Ecological Rationality, Institutions and the Management of Common Property Resources' 31(2) (2000) *Development and Change* at 361-383

[37] World Bank *World Development Report 2002: Building Institutions for Markets* (Oxford Press, 2002).

[38] International Development Association (IDA) 'IDA at Work: Building Strong Institutions for Sustained Results' available at https://ida.worldbank.org/sites/default/files/pdfs/ida-at-work-building-strong-institutions.pdf accessed on 16/01/2020.

[39] McKenzie Johnson 'Strong Institutions in Weak States: Institution Building, Natural Resource Governance, and Conflict in Ghana and Sierra Leone' PhD thesis, Duke University (2017) at 12.

[40] See also Mamadou Dia *Africa's Management in the 1990s and Beyond: Reconciling Indigenous and Transplanted Institutions* (World Bank, 1996).

[41] Ashish Aggarwal 'Indigenous Institutions for Natural Resource Management: Potential and Threats' 43(23) (2008) *Economic & Political Weekly*, 21-24 at 23.

[42] Jeremy de Beer, Kun Fu & Sacha Wunsch-Vincent 'Innovation in the informal economy' in Erica Kraemer-Mbula & Sacha Wunsch-Vincent (eds.) *The Informal Economy in Developing Nations-Hidden engine of innovation?* (Cambridge University Press, 2016) at 73.

[43] OECD & Eurostat, *Oslo Manual: Guidelines for Collecting and Interpreting Innovation Data* (Paris: OECD Publications, 2005) at 46.

[44] Jacques Charmes, Fred Gault & Sacha Wunsch-Vincent 'Formulating an Agenda for the Measurement of Innovation in the Informal Economy' in Erica Kraemer-Mbula & Sacha Wunsch-Vincent (eds.) *The Informal Economy in Developing Nations-Hidden engine of innovation?* (Cambridge University Press, 2016) at 338

[45] Luiz Carlos Beduschi, Raúl Contreras & Raúl Holz 'Innovation for sustainable rural development' FAO (2017) at 2.

[46] The others are a regulatory and policy framework; entrepreneurial ecosystem and access to finance; human capital; and technical and R&D infrastructure. See UNCTAD 'Technology and Innovation Report 2018-Harnessing frontier technologies for sustainable development' (2018) at 55.

[47] Oguamanam Chidi 'Tiered or Differentiated Approach to Traditional Knowledge and Traditional Cultural Expressions: The Evolution of a Concept,' CIGI Papers No. 185 (2018) at 5

[48] See also Article 8(j), *Convention on Biological Diversity*, 1760 UNTS 79 (1992).

[49] See Erica Kraemer-Mbula & Sacha Wunsch-Vincent (eds.) *The Informal Economy in Developing Nations-Hidden engine of innovation?* (Cambridge University Press, 2016) at xxvi.

[50] Stephen Oluwatobi, Uchenna Efobi, Isaiah Olurinola & Philip Alege 'Innovation in Africa: why institutions matter?' (2015) *South African Journal of Economics* at 2

[51] UNCTAD 'Pro-poor technology, innovation and entrepreneurship

policies' UNCTAD/B/C. II/MEM.1/12, Geneva, 16-18 January 2012 at 11.

[52] Elizabeth Hoffecker, 'Local Innovation: what it is and why it matters for developing economies' Working Paper 01, May 2018 at 2

[53] The other context is within peer-to-peer networks of product users (also described as open, horizontal or user innovation. Open innovation 'transcends organization and locational boundaries, relying instead on digital connectivity to link participants in the innovation process across disparate locales'

[54] Britta Rutert and Cath Traynor 'Complexities of Social Innovation and Social Entrepreneurship by Two Indigenous Organisations in Rural South Africa' Open Air, Working Paper 20 (2019).

[55] Bureau of European Policy Advisers (BEPA) 'Empowering People, Driving Change: Social Innovation in the European Union' (European Communities, 2011)

[56] Geoff Mulgan, Simon Tucker, Rushanara Ali, and Ben Sanders 'Social Innovation: What it is, Why it Matters, and How it can be Accelerated' Skoll Centre for Social Entrepreneurship, Working Paper (2007) at 8-10.

[57] Jussi Jauhiainen and Lauri Hooli, 'Indigenous Knowledge and Developing Countries' Innovation Systems: The Case of Namibia,' 1(1) (2017) *International Journal of Innovation Studies* 89-106 at 92.

[58] Richard Heeks, Mirta Amalia, Robert Kintu & Nishant Shah 'Inclusive Innovation: Definition, Conceptualisation and Future Research Priorities' *Manchester Centre for Development Informatics Working Paper* 53 (2013) at 2.

[59] Elizabeth Sumida Huaman 'Indigenous-Minded Innovation in Shifting Ecologies' in Elizabeth Sumida Huaman & Bharath Sriraman (eds.), *Indigenous Innovation: Universalities and Peculiarities*, (SensePublishers, Rotterdam, 2015) at 1-10.

[60] WIPO 'The Protection of Traditional Knowledge: Outline of Policy Options and Legal Elements' WIPO/GRTKF/IC/7/6, para 17

[61] Republic of Kenya *The National Policy on Traditional Knowledge, Genetic Resources and Traditional Cultural Expressions* (Government of Kenya, 2009) 1.

[62] Asli Kunt, 'What Explains Firm Innovation in Developing Countries?', available at http://blogs.worldbank.org/allaboutfinance/what-explains-firm-innovation-developing-countries, accessed on 30/11/2019.

[63] Michaela Trippl 'Regional Innovation Systems and Knowledge-sourcing Activities in Traditional Industries – Evidence from the Vienna Food Sector' (2011) 43(7) *Environment and Planning A*, 1599-1616 at 1599

[64] Stelios Michalopoulos and Elias Papaioannou 'Pre-colonial Ethnic Institutions and Contemporary African Development' (2013) 81 *Econometrica* at 117.

[65] Desmond Oriakhogba 'Empowering Rural Women Crafters in KwaZulu-Natal: The dynamics of intellectual property, traditional cultural expressions, innovation and social entrepreneurship' (2020)137 *The South African Law Journal* at 145-172.

[66] The others are national entrepreneurship strategy; education and skills; innovation and technology; access to finance; and awareness and networking. See UNCTAD 'UNCTAD Entrepreneurship Policy Framework and its implementation' (2013) available at https://unctad.org/en/Pages/DIAE/

Entrepreneurship/EPF-4.aspx accessed on 02/01/2020.

[67] UNCTAD 'The Least Developed Countries Report 2018-Entrepreneurship for structural transformation: Beyond business as usual' (2018) at 14.

[68] Niels Bosma, Jeroen Content, Mark Sanders & Erik Stam 'Institutions, Entrepreneurship, and Economic Growth in Europe' 51(2) (2018) *Small Business Economics* at 483.

[69] See also Brendan Tobin 'Bridging the Nagoya Compliance Gap: The Fundamental Role of Customary Law in Protection of Indigenous Peoples' Resource and Knowledge Rights' (2013) 9(2) *Law Environment and Development Journal*, 142-162 at 151-153.

[70] Rochelle Spencer, Martin Brueckner, Gareth Wise & Marika Bundak 'Capacity Development and Indigenous Social Enterprise: The Case of the Rirratjingu Clan in Northeast Arnhem Land' (2017) 23 *Journal of Management & Organization* at 841.

[71] Tatiana Thieme 'Turning Hustlers into Entrepreneurs, and Social Needs into Market Demands: Corporate–Community Encounters in Nairobi, Kenya' (2015) 59 *Geoforum* at 230

[72] Kari Koskinen 'Inclusive Innovation in the Private Sector: The Case of East African Technology Start-Ups' (2017) *Proceedings of the 50th Hawaii International Conference on System Sciences*, 4159-4168 at 4162.

[73] UNCTAD 'The Least Developed Countries Report 2018-Entrepreneurship for structural transformation: Beyond business as usual' (2018) at 13.

[74] International Fund for Agricultural Development (IFAD) 'The Traditional Knowledge Advantage: Indigenous peoples' knowledge in climate change adaptation and mitigation strategies' (2016) at 7.

[75] Open Communique from the Indigenous Data Sovereignty Summit, Canberra, ACT, to all individuals involved in data and data infrastructure in Australia, *Indigenous Data Sovereignty* (June 20, 2018) available at https://perma.cc/8VPR-9TTL accessed on 12/12/2020.

[76] Chidi Oguamanam 'Indigenous Data Sovereignty: Retooling Indigenous Resurgence Development' CIGI Papers No. 234 (2019) at 8.

[77] See also Rebecca Tsosie 'Tribal Data Governance and Informational Privacy: Constructing "Indigenous Data Sovereignty" 80(2) (2019) *Montana Law Review* at 230.

[78] See also Nicolas Gorjestani 'Indigenous Knowledge for Development' available at https://www.google.com/url?sa=t&rct=j&q=&esrc=s&source=web&cd=1&cad=rja&uact=8&ved=2ahUKEwjdpfaApZHlAhVB2AKHSSAB68QFjAAegQIABAB&url=http%3A%2F%2Fweb.worldbank.org%2Farchive%2Fwebsite00297C%2FWEB%2FIMAGES%2FIKPAPER_.PDF&usg=AOvVaw2kFdKUZvXetZEktv7dHpZH, accessed on 25/09/ 2019.

[79] Grant Isaac & William Kerr 'Bioprospecting or Biopiracy: Intellectual Property and Traditional Knowledge in Biotechnology Innovation' (2005) 7 *The Journal of World Intellectual Property*, 35-52 at 36.

[80] Interview with Mbeere traditional potters on 12/11/2019.

[81] Interview with the General Coordinator of ABN at Thika on 14/10/2019.

[82] Workshop with women potters in Mbeere held on 13/11/2019.

[83] Angela Langenkamp 'Structural Changes of the Potters Craft in Kenya: A Regional and Gender-based Disparities' PhD Thesis, Universitätsverlag Rasch Osnabrück (2000).

[84] Patrick A. Kafu & Genevieve N. Simwelo 'Forest conservation in Kenya: Lessons from the African Traditional/ Indigenous Education' (2015) 5(8) *Developing Country Studies* 140-144 at 142.

[85] A workshop with *kaya* elders on 22/04/2018.

[86] Meeting with *kaya* elders at Kaloleni, Kilifi on 05/11/2019.

[87] A meeting with the director of Natural Justice in Kenya on 06/11/2019.

[88] Interview with Caxton Mwanyenje, CEO Careway-Trust on 05/11/2019.

[89] Care Way-Trust inventories, document with author.

[90] Institute for Culture and Ecology (ICE) 'Documentation of traditional and ecological laws of Tharaka' undated report, 14 available at https://www.icekenya.org/publications/ accessed on 20/06/2018.

[91] Mark Bevir *Governance: A Very Short Introduction* (Oxford University Press, 2012) at 1.

[92] Jeremy de Beer 'Ownership of Open Data: Governance Options for Agriculture and Nutrition' Global Open Data for Agriculture and Nutrition Report) (2016) at 7.

[93] Chisa and Ruth Hoskins 'African customary law and the protection of indigenous cultural heritage: Challenges and issues in the digitization of indigenous knowledge in South Africa' (2016) 15 *African Journal of Indigenous Knowledge Systems,* 1-15 at 4.

[94] Francis Kariuki 'Traditional justice systems as *sui generis* frameworks for the protection of traditional ecological knowledge in Kenya' PhD thesis, University of the Witwatersrand (2019), 218-225.

[95] Interview with a *kaya* elder at Kaloleni on 04/11/2019.

[96] Interview with a *kaya* elder from *kaya* Kambe at Kaloleni on 04/11/2019.

Section 3

Methodology and Application

Chapter 5

A Methodology for Evaluation and Distribution of Patent Applications to INPI-BR Patent Examiners: A Case Study in the Electricity Field

Cesar Vianna Moreira Júnior, Daniel Marques Golodne and Ricardo Carvalho Rodrigues

Abstract

This paper presents the development of a new methodology for evaluation and distribution of patent applications to the examiners at the Brazilian Patent Office considering a specific technological field, represented by classification of the application according to the International Patent Classification (IPC), and the variables corresponding to the volume of data of the application and its complexity for the examination process. After identifying the most relevant variables, such as the Specific Areas of Expertise (ZAE) of the examiners, a mathematical model was developed, including: (a) application of the principal component analysis (PCA) method; (b) calculation of a General Complexity Ratio (IGC); (c) classification into five classes (very light, light, moderate, heavy and very heavy) according to IGC average ranges and standard deviations; (d) implementation of a logic of distribution, compensating very heavy applications with very light ones, and light applications with heavy ones; and (e) calculation of a Distribution Balancing Ratio (IBD), considering the differences between the samples' medians. The model was validated using a sample of patent applications including, in addition to the identified variables, the time for substantive examination by the examiner. Then, a correlation analysis of the variables with time and a comparison of the classifications according to the time and the IGC generated by the model were carried out. The results obtained showed a high correlation of the IGC with time, above 80%, as well as correct IGC classes in more than 80% of applications. The model proposed herein suggests that the three main relevant variables are: total number of pages, total number of claims, and total number of claim pages.

Keywords: Patents, Applications, Evaluation, Distribution, Volume data, IPC, Examiner

1. Introduction

The granting of industrial property (IP) assets should be based on two central and interrelated principles: quality and efficiency. An efficient system to ensure protection of IP rights is basically bound to the time taken to execute the granting procedures, but also to the clarity and organization of the analysis performed during the technical examination. On its turn, quality is usually bound to the standardization and improvement of administrative proceedings, providing reliability and legal certainty in decisions.

As to the granting procedures and time for granting industrial property rights, the Brazilian National Institute of Industrial Property – INPI-BR has been using its efforts to significantly reduce and adjust the granting time taken by the Institute to the average of major international offices. Among its actions, we note the implementation of the so-called "backlog combat plan" announced still in 2019, which is already in effect and expected to be in place until 2021 [1]. It is also worth highlighting the results and efforts regarding the time taken by the Institute to register trademarks, leading to the inclusion of INPI-BR among the signatories of the Madrid Protocol [2].

Over the last decades, INPI-BR has been incorporating to its Strategic Plan several initiatives related to the quality of its applications/registrations. The Strategic Plan 2018-2021 [3] provided for partnerships, cooperation agreements with international offices, improvement of prioritized examination programs, implementation and review of patent examination guidelines, among other activities. As to the technical cooperation initiatives, we note a recent strategic partnership between INPI-BR and the European Patent Office – EPO that includes training, discussion of best practices, sharing of tools, and exchange of patent databases [4].

It is important to highlight that there are studies [5–7] showing that changes in the workload of examiners can affect the quality of the examination process and its results, suggesting that a factor with high potential of causing instability in the applications/registrations and discrepancies in the decisions of a patent office is the unbalanced workload of patent examiners, i.e., an uneven distribution of patent applications among them. Additionally, it is also relevant to highlight that a specific study [8] using automatically data related to INPI-BR applications showed that the volume of patent applications can be used as a measure of examiner's workload, and suggests that claim's pages is probably a key workload indicator. Such facts become even more relevant since INPI-BR currently does not apply a well defined application distribution method, and the decision/responsibility for distribution is on behalf of the team leaders, who are somewhat free to apply their own criteria.

Thus, due to the importance of the subject for INPI-BR itself, specifically for the Patent Directorate of the Brazilian National Institute of Industrial Property – DIRPA, and to the scarcity of studies on methods for analyzing and distributing patent applications to the examiners, aiming at balancing the workload in an optimized manner, the development of a method in this regard would be a great contribution to the efficiency and quality of patent examination, being an important element to fulfill the mission of international Intellectual Property offices in general.

2. Patent document and the variables of interest to evaluate the distribution

2.1 Basic structure of patent applications

The Brazilian Industrial Property Law (LPI) [9], in its chapter III – article 19, defines that a patent application shall include: application; description; claims; figures, if any; abstract; and proof of payment of the application fee. Therefore, disregarding the abstract, which is usually limited to a single page, a patent application is basically composed of three major parts: description, patent claims, and figures (whenever necessary). We note that these three main parts have specific shape and content characteristics that should be evaluated in more details.

2.1.1 Description

Regarding the description, article 24 of the LPI provides that: "The description shall describe the object clearly and sufficiently, as to enable reproduction by an expert, and indicate, when applicable, the best mode of execution.".

Thus, the description includes the details of the applicant/inventor's invention, clearly explaining its practical implementation to third parties and a person skilled in the art. Consequently, it is one of the most relevant parts of the patent application and is expected to have more pages. Therefore, the number of pages of description of a patent application is a variable relevant to its evaluation.

2.1.2 Claims

Regarding claims, article 25 of the LPI provides that: "The claims shall be based on the description, describe the particularities of the application, and provide a clear and accurate definition of the subject matter of the protection".

We note that, within a same patent claim's section, the claims may be classified as independent or dependent. Independent claims seek to protect essential and specific technical characteristics of the invention as a whole, while dependent claims are those that, while keeping the unity of invention, include all features of other previous claim(s) and define details of these characteristics and/or additional characteristics not deemed essential to the invention [10].

Therefore, according to the comprehensive content in the description, the claims specify, on a more accurate basis, the object of protection, i.e., define the scope of protection. In a recent study [11], the role of the characterizing term (the expression "characterized by") in the patent documentation for delimitation of industrial property rights is discussed in more details considering the history of the Brazilian and international legal framework.

In this context, we note that both the extent of the claims (number of patent claim pages) and the number of claims (total number of independent and dependent claims) are highly relevant to the examination of a patent application.

2.1.3 Figures

As provided for in article 19 of the LPI, the submission of drawings/figures in the patent application is optional. While the figures are not mandatory, we note that the majority of applicants and inventors include them in the documentation submitted for examination. Such fact points that figures are an important part of the patent application, and one of the main reasons therefor is that they facilitate reading and understanding of the subject matter under examination. Hence, the number of figures pages can also be relevant when examining a patent application.

2.2 Cover sheet: bibliographic data of the patent documentation

Information included in patent documentation (including bibliographic data in the cover sheet) is an important tool for technological research and development [12]. It is important to note that information included in the cover sheet of a patent document is identified by numeric codes, as the Internationally Agreed Numbers for the Identification of Data (INID), and its specific standards are defined by the World Intellectual Property Organization – WIPO.

Among the bibliographic data included in the cover sheet, we highlight: application number (21), number of the priority document, if any (31); filing date (22); priority date, if any (32); date of publication (43); name of the inventor (72); name of the holder of the rights on the patent (73); International Patent Classification (51); title of the invention (54); and abstract (57). A detailed description of these codes can be found in Appendix 1 of Standard ST.9 of the WIPO Handbook on Industrial Property Information and Documentation [13].

In this context, it is important to highlight that, as we intend to obtain variables relevant for evaluating and distributing patent applications for examination, among these bibliographic data, we are only interested in those already available from the filing until publication of the application, i.e., those that can be obtained before the patent examination process. Thus, in a first analysis, we focus on the identification numbers of the applications, filing date/year, inventors, priorities, and international patent classification (IPC), provided that the latter will be addressed in further details below.

2.3 International patent classification (IPC)

The IPC [14] allowed for standardization of documents from different countries with different languages and technical expressions. Pursuant to WIPO, it has an important role as it serves as: (i) an instrument for the orderly arrangement of patent documents aiming to facilitate access to the technological and legal information contained therein; (ii) a basis for selective dissemination of information to all users of patent information as a reference and/or knowledge; (iii) a basis for investigating the state of the art in given fields of technology; (iv) a basis for the preparation of industrial property statistics which in turn allows the assessment of technological development in various areas [15].

The IPC is divided into eight sections (A, B, C, D, E, F, G, and H). The sections are the highest levels of hierarchy of the classification. Each section is subdivided into classes, representing the second hierarchical level of the classification. Each class comprises one or more subclasses, indicating the third hierarchical level of the classification. Each subclass is broken down into subdivisions, referred to as "groups", which are either main groups (fourth hierarchical level of the classification) or subgroups (lower hierarchical levels dependent upon the main group level of the classification). We present below an example classification of the electricity area by using all hierarchical levels, from section to subgroup.

Example: H02M 7/48.

Where:

H Section (A, B, [...], H): Electricity;

H02 Class (two digits): Energy Production, Conversion, or Distribution;

H02M Subclass (one letter): Apparatus for Conversion Between DC and AC;

H02M7 Main Group (one or more numeric digits): Conversion of AC power input into DC power output;

H02M7/48 Subgroup – (at least two numeric digits): using discharge tubes with control electrode or semiconductor devices with control electrode.

We highlight that the IPC is revised periodically based on meetings with experts from WIPO member countries, and such revision is published and may be accessed through INPI and WIPO websites. We further highlight that a patent document may fall under more than one IPC symbol. This is due to the fact that it can have claims in more than one category (device and method, for example), be related to one or more areas of application, or even to specific functions.

The study of Harloff and Wagner [16], based on EPO data for modeling the examination time, defined that, among other factors that impact the complexity of a patent application, the total number of claims and the number of IPC subclasses are major direct variables of the application. Therefore, the number of IPC subclasses is also a variable to be considered when evaluating a patent application to be distributed.

2.4 Studies using variables of patent documentation

2.4.1 Miscellaneous studies

As seen previously, a patent application is basically composed of three main parts: description, claims and figures (if any). For description and figures, for example, the number of pages is a relevant variable. As for patent claims, the number of pages, number of claims, whether independent or not, etc. Additionally, bibliographic data present information that also become potentially relevant variables, such as IPC classification, inventors, filing dates and years, etc. In this context, there are some papers that use specific variables of patent documentation to determine specifications like: economic value, time effort applied to the technical evaluation, scope of patent protection, among others.

An economic value approach to European patents using their claims, references, among others as variables, is described in [17].

Other papers [18, 19] are related to methods for analyzing and assessing the scope of protection of a patent based on variables related to the patent claim scope. The first uses the number of pages of the first independent patent claim as a relevant variable. The second uses two variables: the number of words in the shortest independent patent claim and the total number of independent claims.

However, none of the papers mentioned address the use of the parameters of the patent application or data in the examination process to create a method for distributing the applications to examiners. In [20, 21], studies were carried out with evidence that, at the United States Patent and Trademark Office –USPTO, after the application was directed to a large technological area (for example, electricity or chemistry), its subsequent designation to a specific examiner was nearly random. On the other hand, [22] found evidence that, at USPTO, applications of the same applicant, as well as applications with similar abstracts and titles, tend to be distributed to the same examiner. The authors suggest that, although such methods seek to follow the principle of efficiency, a balance with the principle of justice should be pursued as well. On the other hand, they emphasize that a random distribution favors the principle of justice, but fails to follow the principle of efficiency, which counts on the expertise of the examiners in certain examination subclasses.

In view of the foregoing, one has to take into account not only factors contributing to efficiency, such as distribution of application by subclasses pursuant to the examiners' education/interest, but also factors contributing to better balance, i.e., variables including the amount of data and the complexity of the patent applications to be examined. Consequently, justice should not be confused with randomness.

2.4.2 Workload balancing, voluminosity, and complexity of patent applications

As already seen, the workload in each patent office is one of the indicators affecting the quality not only of patent examination, but of patent systems as a whole. It is also worth mentioning that the increased workload of examiners, and the consequent decrease in time for examining a patent application, may adversely affect the quality of patents granted, i.e., it tends to increase the granting of improper patents. Thus, it is important to seek better workload distribution and balancing to the examiners, as to reconcile working conditions and results.

Papers [23, 24] show that the volume of patent applications at EPO has been increasing throughout the years, and they relate the volume of patent application to an essentially two-dimensional problem, with two predominant variables: total number of pages of the patent application and number of claims. In this context, the total number of pages would be related to the level of description of the invention at stake and the total number of claims to protection scope. The authors also emphasize that these variables would be correlated, in different proportions, to the number of priorities, inventors, and IPC classifications. As limitations to the study, they mention that it would be better to evaluate the amount of independent and dependent claims, although this information is not easily accessible in data sources available.

To assess the hypothesis of technological complexity of a patent application, another study [25] uses a mathematical model considering the number of inventors, the number of IPC classes, and the number of references to previous patents. The authors emphasize that the increased volume of data may be related to both the technical complexity of the invention/application and a strategy matter, i.e., the desire to maintain certain know-how rather than actually protect it. It is important to highlight that, with the results of the model applied, the authors suggest that an increased number of inventors tend to create more complex inventions, requiring a greater number of pages and claims so that such inventions are described in details.

2.5 Substantive patent examination: main steps and related variables

2.5.1 Step 1: initial technical analysis

When the examiner receives a new patent application for examination, it is clear that the first step, which may takes a longer time, is reading the application. In principle, as the examiner needs to carefully read the entire application and see the figures, further confirming if the claims are based in the description and if the matter is sufficiently described so that a third person skilled in the art can execute it, the relevant variable to be considered in this step is the application's total number of pages.

2.5.2 Step 2: prior art search

Upon the Initial Technical Analysis, the examiner should carry a prior art search aiming at determining the state-of-the-art closer to the matter claimed. For the searches, the examiner should basically consider the patent claim scope, more specifically its independent claims. Additionally, if the claims include several specifications and are quite extensive, an even greater effort shall be employed. Finally, the greater the number of classifications in the application, the greater the tendency to address more than one technological area or borderline regions, which can also cause the search to be even more complex. Thus, the number of independent claims, the number of pages of the patent claims, and the number of subclasses of the application may also be variables to be considered in this step.

2.5.3 Step 3: specific technical analysis

Upon searches and determination of the useful prior art for examination, the third major step is the comparison between the matter claimed and the knowledge presented in the state-of-the-art, i.e., analysis of the patentability. This third step is hereinafter referred to as Specific Technical Analysis. Upon analysis of patentability, a detailed examination of the independent claims in the application is mandatory. Thus, the first relevant variable in this step will be the number of independent claims. As in the searches, if the claims are quite extensive and have several technical specifications, the effort applied will be greater. So the number of claim pages is also a relevant variable in this step. As in some cases, dependent claims are also analyzed in details, the possibility of using the number of dependent claims is considered, and, in this case, the total number of claims could be used as a variable of interest.

2.6 Selected variables and initial hypotheses

Twelve possible variables were initially identified to be used in this paper: number of pages of description (Variable 1); number of claim pages (Variable 2); number of pages of figures (Variable 3); number of third parties observation pages (Variable 4); number of independent claims (Variable 5); number of dependent claims (Variable 6); number of IPC subclasses (Variable 7); year of filing (Variable 8); number of inventors (Variable 9); number of priorities (Variable 10); number of references to the state-of-the-art in the patent document under examination (Variable 11); number of references to the patent document under examination in other patent documents (Variable 12).

Upon identification of the possible variables of interest, the following additional criteria were established for selecting study variables:

- moment of availability of the variable - as the main objective is to evaluate the document for later distribution for examination, only variables accessible from filing until publication of the patent application will be selected;

- reliability and efficiency - variables failing to provide full reliability in data obtained, which may require the use of more than one platform/database and/or which require a very long time to be obtained, which could greatly increase the complexity of the model or even render its practical application unfeasible, will not be selected.

It should be noted that most of patent applications filed in INPI only include references to the state-of-the-art after a first examination, i.e., after the application has already been distributed, and references to other documents would still require access to more than one database. In this context, these variables are not deemed to fully meet the criteria of "moment of availability" and "reliability and efficiency". Thus, at first, the variables related to references will be disregarded, hence ten variables will be used to obtain data samples, which are: number of pages of description (Variable 1); number of claim pages (Variable 2); number of pages of figures (Variable 3); number of third parties observation pages (Variable 4); number of independent claims (Variable 5); number of dependent claims (Variable 6); number of IPC subclasses (Variable 7); year of filing (Variable 8); number of inventors (Variable 9); and number of priorities (Variable 10).

Based on the studies carried out with EPO data on voluminosity (volume of data) of a patent application, it appears that the volume of data that the examiner needs to deal with during the examination of a patent application is one of the main constraints on examination effort/time. Additionally, such studies indicate that voluminosity is a problem related to two patent application variables: total number of pages and total number of claims. Thus, a first assumption will consider that the volume of data of a patent application can be represented by the variables with the greatest positive correlation with the total number of pages of the application and/or with the total number of claims. Initial hypothesis 1 is that there are five variables directly bound to the volume of data: number of pages of description, claim pages, and pages of figures, in addition to the number of dependent and independent claims.

On the other hand, although most of the examination effort is bound to the direct volume of data that the examiner deals with, it is possible to note that there is still the hypothesis of existence of complementary variables, bound to an indirect and more subjective complexity, specifically related to the patent application itself, the applicants' strategy, or even particularities of the examination process. In this context, there are some variables suggested in the studies carried out; however, there is no consensus by the authors or in the studies carried out revealing the exact influence of each of them, if any. Initial hypothesis 2 is that there is, even if reduced, indirect influence of the other abovementioned variables.

3. Methodology

The proposed methodology aims at creating a model capable of evaluating the complexity and volume of patent applications, in addition to a new fair and efficient manner of distributing patent applications to patent examiners. For this, it is necessary to obtain the application data with its variables of interest, evaluate patent applications according to the selected variables, create a specific logic for this distribution, and, finally, evaluate the new proposed logic compared to the original distribution. Thus, the proposed method can be divided into four main parts, which complement each other and will be detailed below.

3.1 Evaluation of patent applications as to volume of data and complexity: initial tests

We obtained data from applications that already went through the first examination step during two years, in the area of electricity, more precisely from May 2015 to May 2017, month in which the research was initiated. By identifying and selecting the variables, the proposal was to tabulate data from all patent applications analyzed, including all relevant variables selected, and identify the patent examiner who received the application for analysis. These data were defined as the Initial Test Sample and, based on it, the IPC for the sample patent applications and, consequently, the specific area of expertise (ZAE) of each examiner were then identified.

As this is a problem with multiple variables of interest, we attempted to find a multivariate analysis method to solve it. The bibliographic review was made to choose a method that meets the following criteria:

- did not limit the number of variables used;
- was based on a pair correlation analysis of each variable in order to enable a specific analysis of their relations;
- in case of a high number of variables, allowed for reduction of the size of the problem, i.e., to reduce the number of variables (n) to other components or variables (x), with $x < n$, without significant loss of data or of information about the problem to be resolved; and

- was mathematically and statistically robust and scientifically tested in many different fields of knowledge.

Given the established criteria, the method of principal component analysis (PCA) was selected as the basic tool for evaluation of patent applications. Such method allows for determination of such principal components of the specific problem according to the share of general variance explained by each of the components. Following identification of these new components, a General Complexity Ratio (IGC) is proposed for the patent applications, which is the ratio of the weighted sum of the most significant components plus their eigenvalues to the sum of the eigenvalues themselves, which were obtained from the correlation matrix of the original variables of the problem. Based on these ratios for each of the applications, these were classified into up to five classes (Very Light, Light, Moderate, Heavy, and Very Heavy) according to the average and the standard deviation of the general ratios obtained. It is important to highlight that the eigenvalues and eigenvectors were determined both manually and with the assistance of the software Matlab and of the Matrix Calculator (Available at https://matrixcalc.org/pt/vectors.html), and the other steps were executed using Excel electronic spreadsheets (Microsoft Office 2010).

3.2 Evaluation of patent applications as to volume of data and complexity: validation tests with time

After choosing the method, determining the ratios and the classification of the applications into classes, the next step is a sensitivity analysis/validation of the ratios and classification of the patent applications. For this step, an experimental/empirical research is proposed, aiming to establish a correlation between the ratios and classifications found and the time/effort to exam the patent applications. First, the substantive process of patent examination by INPI and the standard examination report were analyzed in order to identify the main examination steps and directly or indirectly related variables. Based on these main examination steps, a form was prepared to survey the time for examination, to be filled up by the examiners, in which information about the time to execute each step is inserted. Thus, a list of applications is determined, hereinafter referred to as Standard Sample, with tabulation of data, including all the variables of interest in addition to the time for examination. The PCA method will then be applied to this new sample, and the IGC ratios for each patent application will be calculated, in addition to their classification into classes. In this context, the correlation between the ratios obtained and the time for examination will be verified, and the PCA method will be applied, including several simulations with variations in the sample size and in the number of variables. This procedure aims at showing the variables with direct impact on the time for examination and the representativeness of the IGC regarding these variables, evaluating the minimum necessary sample size, and also testing the applicability of the PCA method.

3.3 Distribution of patent applications

In this 3rd part of the proposed method, a specific logic for distribution of applications was built based on the previously obtained classification into the five classes, and also on the classification of the application according to the IPC. Data obtained from the patent applications were separated by main IPC subclasses, and so, the main subclasses examined by each examiner were identified, as well as their ZAE was determined. This area was obtained considering the subclasses of patent applications with occurrences above 5% of the total examinations by each examiner evaluated based on the largest sample obtained, the Initial Test Sample. Thus, a new logic of distribution of patent applications is proposed according to the classification of the general ratios and to the ZAE, considering the following criteria:

- Very heavy and heavy applications shall be equally distributed among the examiners;
- Very heavy and heavy applications shall be compensated, respectively, with distribution of very light and light applications;
- The remaining moderate applications shall be distributed;
- In all previous steps, patent applications shall be distributed considering the ZAE determined for each examiner.

3.4 Evaluation of the new distribution logic

In the fourth and last part of the proposed method, first a new sample of more recent patent applications was obtained, hereinafter referred to as the Final Redistribution Sample. Patent application data were obtained from the same examiners in the field of electricity that made up the Initial Test Sample, however, with the first examinations carried out between May and July 2020. It is important to note that, after the backlog combat plan was implemented by INPI, the examination process has somewhat changed for most of the patent applications in the area of electricity. Hence, obtaining this redistribution sample was necessary to harmonize the examination process carried out by the examiners evaluated therein with the process implemented by the examiner, from which the Standard Sample with time was obtained. This harmonization was made using standard samples with time and redistribution samples containing the same type of patent applications, in other words, patent applications that may be examined using data from previous searches by international offices. It is important to note that this type of application covers an average of 88% of the total stock of patent applications filed until 2016 in the field of electricity.

Based on this new sample, we apply the proposed model and logic for distribution, and then calculate a Distribution Balancing Ratio (IBD) both for the original distribution and for the new distribution, a ratio that ranges from zero to one, and considers the differences between the medians of the variables of each examiner's samples and the general medians of the division's variables. Within this context, it should be noted that the closer the medians of the variables of the examiners' individual samples are to the general medians of the division's variables, the larger the amount of the IDB is and, consequently, the better balanced the distribution is. The breakdown of the IBD, including explanations and analyses about its formula, maximum and minimum limits, will be presented in item 4 – Development.

4. Development

4.1 Principal component analysis (PCA)

The principal component analysis is a multivariate statistics technique focused on explaining the variance–covariance structure of a set of data, and its main objectives are the reduction of the dimensionality of the problem and the better interpretation of data [26–28]. Still according to [27], the PCA usually reveals relations that would not have been previously identified only with an analysis of the original set of data and variables, enabling a more comprehensive interpretation of the study phenomenon.

To examine a patent application, several measured variables of each patent application of the study population should be considered. The proposal of the principal component analysis method is to apply a transformation to such variables, so that the new components obtained enable a better breakdown and analysis of the elements of such population. In [29], it is shown that this new look has great value when it comes to creating a typology for the population, classifying the elements according to certain criteria, etc. According to Vicini [30] "In practice, the algorithm is based on the variance-covariance matrix, or on the correlation matrix, from which the eigenvalues and eigenvectors are extracted" and "finally, writing the linear combinations, which will be the new variables, referred to as principal components".

It is important to note that the PCA is widely employed, evidencing its efficiency and robustness in applications in several fields of knowledge, such as agronomy, zootechnics, medicine, among others [31–34]. Examples of practical applications of the PCA for evaluation of public services in Brazilian states, assessment of the regional development of cities in the Brazilian state of Santa Catarina, as well as analysis of crime statistics in U.S. states can be found, respectively, in the papers [35–37].

The following steps are necessary for determining the principal components:

1. create an original data matrix X_{ij} of size n x p in which the columns (j = 1, 2, ..., p) are the original variables of the problem and the rows (i = 1, 2, ..., n) are individuals in the population (in our case, each patent application);

2. standardize the original variables so all of them have mean equal to zero and standard deviation equal to one, avoiding the influence of different orders of magnitude and obtaining a new data matrix Z_{ij};

3. calculate the variance–covariance matrix (S) and the correlation matrix (R) which, in case of standardized variables, will be equal;

4. find the eigenvalues of the matrices and their corresponding eigenvectors;

5. select the components calculating linear combinations of original variables with the eigenvectors of the correlation matrix.

Eqs. (1) and (2) below show, respectively, the calculation for standardization of the variables and matrix Z of standardized variables.

$$Z_{ij} = \frac{X_{ij} - \mu_p}{\delta_p} \tag{1}$$

$$Z = \begin{bmatrix} Z_{11} & Z_{12} & \cdots & Z_{1p} \\ Z_{21} & Z_{22} & \cdots & Z_{2p} \\ \vdots & \vdots & \ddots & \vdots \\ Z_{n1} & Z_{n2} & \cdots & Z_{nn} \end{bmatrix} \tag{2}$$

Where: X_{ij} is the element of the original data matrix; μ_p is the average of variable p, being p = j; and δ_p is the standard deviation of variable p, being p = j.

Eqs. (3)-(5) below show, respectively, the calculation of the variances, covariances, and matrix S.

$$VAR[Z_j] = \frac{1}{n}\sum_{k=1}^{n}\left(Z_{jk} - \mu_j\right)^2 \tag{3}$$

$$COV\left[Z_j; Z_{j'}\right] = \frac{1}{n}\sum_{k=1}^{n}\left[\left(Z_{jk} - \mu_j\right)\left(Z_{j'k} - \mu_{j'}\right)\right] \tag{4}$$

$$S = \begin{bmatrix} VAR[Z_1;Z_1] & COV[Z_1;Z_2] & \dots & COV[Z_1;Z_p] \\ COV[Z_2;Z_1] & VAR[Z_2;Z_2] & \dots & COV[Z_2;Z_p] \\ \vdots & \vdots & \ddots & \vdots \\ COV[Z_p;Z_1] & COV[Z_p;Z_2] & \dots & VAR[Z_p;Z_p] \end{bmatrix} = \begin{bmatrix} 1 & COV[Z_1;Z_2] & \dots & COV[Z_1;Z_p] \\ COV[Z_2;Z_1] & 1 & \dots & COV[Z_2;Z_p] \\ \vdots & \vdots & \ddots & \vdots \\ COV[Z_p;Z_1] & COV[Z_p;Z_2] & \dots & 1 \end{bmatrix} \tag{5}$$

Where: VAR $[Z_j]$ is the variance of the standardized variable Z_j; COV$[Z_j; Z_j']$ is the covariance of the standardized variables Z_j and Z_j'; n is the number of individuals; μ_j and μ_j' are, respectively, the average of the standardized variables Z_j and Z_j'; and Z_{jk} are the data matrix elements.

Eqs. (6) and (7) below allow for determination of the eigenvalues and eigenvectors of matrix S and, so, matrix V of eigenvectors of S is determined according to Eq. (8).

$$|S - \lambda.I| = 0 \tag{6}$$

$$S.V = \lambda.V \tag{7}$$

$$V = [V1 \quad V2 \quad \cdots \quad Vp\ ] = \begin{bmatrix} v_{11} & v_{12} & \dots & v_{1p} \\ v_{21} & v_{22} & \dots & v_{2p} \\ \vdots & \vdots & \ddots & \vdots \\ v_{p1} & v_{p2} & \dots & v_{pp} \end{bmatrix} \tag{8}$$

Where: S is the Variance–Covariance matrix of pxp dimension of standardized data; λ is one of the p eigenvalues of matrix S; I is the identity matrix of order p; p is the total number of standardized variables; and V is an eigenvector of S with dimension px1;

Upon acquisition of the eigenvectors associated with eigenvalues in a descending order, the principal components (Y_1, Y_2, ... , Y_p) for each of the n individuals under analysis is determined through a linear combination between the standardized variables and the eigenvalues calculated. Therefore, we can then write the components of individual n in the form of the following equation:

$$Y_{i\ (n)} = Z_{i1}.v_{1i} + Z_{i2}.v_{2i} + \cdots + Z_{ip}.v_{pi} \tag{9}$$

Where: i ranges from 1 to p; $Y_{i\ (n)}$ is component i of individual n; Z_{ip} are the elements of matrix Z of standardized variables; and vpi are the elements of the eigenvectors calculated.

It is important to highlight that in the PCA, the contribution of each principal component (Y_1, Y_2, … , Y_p) is measured in terms of its variance. Thus, it is possible to calculate that contribution considering the relation between the variance of the component under analysis and the sum of the variances of all components, resulting in the proportion (or percentage) of total explained variance to each of the components. Eq. (10) below shows how to calculate each contribution C_i (C_1, C_2, … , C_p).

$$C_i = \frac{VAR(Y_i)}{\sum_{i=1}^{p} VAR(Y_i)}.100 = \frac{\lambda_i}{\sum_{i=1}^{p} \lambda_i}.100 \tag{10}$$

Where: C_i is the contribution or total % variance explained by component Y_i; $VAR(Y_i)$ is the variance of principal component Y_i; λ_i is one of p eigenvalues of matrix S; p is the total number of standardized variables.

It should be noted that further details about the PCA formal mathematical statements and its properties, as well as about all linear algebra used, may be consulted throughout the already mentioned works [26–37].

4.2 Selection criteria for principal components

Kaiser's [38] is the most used criterion to date. According to such criterion, only components associated with eigenvalues with ranges wider than the unit are considered principal components, i.e.: $\lambda_i > 1$. However, some practical cases show that only this selection criterion may not properly represent the majority of the total data variance.

A second option is to perform a graphic analysis and verify greater differences among the consecutive eigenvalues. The Cattel [39] criterion, for example, suggests a graphic representation of the range of eigenvalues based on the number of eigenvalues, arranged in an ascending order. The number of components would be selected based on the breaking point of the graph. This breaking point occurs when there is a slump in the range of eigenvalues [40].

A third possible criterion, also quite disseminated, is to use a reference value for the proportion of variance explained by the principal components. Following this logic, the principal components whose cumulative percentage of explained variance exceeds such reference value shall be selected. It is important to highlight that there is no consensus among researchers about which percentage should be used, and there are several practical examples. A great part of the applications uses the limit of 70%. In [40], the problem was ranked in levels of acceptance, and amounts between 62 and 80% were considered reasonable or "partially good".

Although each criterion has advantages and disadvantages, in this paper a combination of the three above-described criteria was adopted. As a reference value for the third criterion, we believe a percentage of explained variance starting at 60% is a suitable amount for selecting the most representative principal components.

4.3 General complexity ratio (IGC)

Hongyu et al. [31] also states that "In order to establish a ratio that enables us to order a set of n objects, according to a criterion defined by a set of m suitable variables, it is necessary to choose the weights of the variables so that they translate information contained in them," provided that, to create a ratio as a linear combination of variables, "it is desirable that this ratio includes the maximum possible information of the set of variables selected for study". According to Sandanielo [41] (*apud* HONGYU, 2015), "a method that creates linear combinations with maximum variance is the principal component analysis".

In this context, this paper intends to, in a first evaluation, use a ratio in one dimension based on the most significant principal components (carefully selected using the selection criteria addressed in item 4.2), weighted by their corresponding eigenvalues. Hence, a General Complexity Ratio (IGC) is defined for the patent applications to be evaluated, according to the following equation:

$$IGC_n = \frac{\sum_{i=1}^{k} Y_i \lambda_i}{\sum_{i=1}^{k} \lambda_i} \tag{11}$$

Where: Y_i are the principal components calculated, λ_i are the eigenvalues calculated, k is the number of principal components selected and n is the patent application evaluated.

4.4 Classification of the patent applications into classes

To group data according to the IGC ratio calculated, the first step was to standardize the original values using Eq. (1) and, therefore, the standard deviation of the IGC sample will always be equal to one. Based on IGC data for all patent applications under examination, classification ranges were then defined as shown in **Figure 1**.

4.5 Mathematical model: diagram and evaluation

After calculating the IGC ratio and classifying the applications, the complete model for evaluating patent applications is created. A diagram of the model is presented in **Figure 2**.

Classes	Ranges
Very Heavy	IGC >3
Heavy	1 < IGC <= 3
Moderate	-1 <= IGC <= 1
Light	-3 <= IGC < -1
Very light	IGC < -3

Figure 1.
Classification of the patent applications into classes.

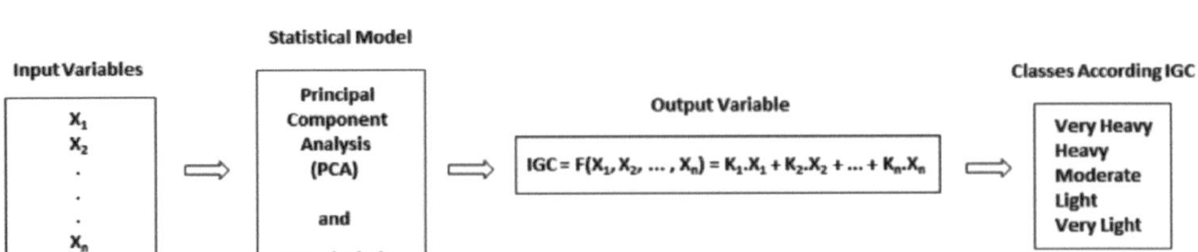

Figure 2.
Diagram of the model.

Thus, the next step is to enable its evaluation through a sensitivity analysis and through the correlations with time for examination/analysis of the application. This evaluation will happen through preparation of a form regarding the time for examination in order to obtain a new Standard Sample of patent applications with time, in addition to several simulations considering different numbers of variables and sample sizes. **Figure 3** shows the template form developed.

4.6 Iterative logic for individual distribution of applications

After classifying all applications to be distributed during the selected period, an iterative sequence of steps for their distribution is then proposed, seeking to prioritize the choice of applications based, whenever possible, on the IGC classification of each application being distributed, in addition to the ZAE of each examiner.

1. Verify the Main IPC Subclass in which the Current Application falls:

    i. If the Current Application pertains to the Current Examiner's ZAE, then select the Current Application and proceed to Step 2;

    ii. If there is no application pertaining to the Current Examiner's ZAE, look for the next application in line that does not pertain to any other Examiner's ZAE and, only after that, proceed to Step 2.

2. Check the Current Application Classification (Very Light, Light, Moderate, Heavy, or Very Heavy):

    i. If an Application with the same Classification has not yet been distributed to the Current Examiner, then distribute the Current Application and proceed to Step 3;

    ii. Otherwise, search for the next available Application and return to Step 1.

3. Repeat Steps 1 and 2 until an Application with each Classification is distributed to the Current Examiner.

4. Go to the next Examiner on the list and perform Steps 1 to 3.

5. Repeat Steps 1 to 4 until there are enough Applications in each of the Classifications:

			Form - information about the time to execute each step of substantive patent exam										
			Step 1: Initial Technical Analysis				Step 2: Prior Art Search			Step 3: Specific Technical Analysis			
			Reading and understanding of the application				Search execution			Analysis of the Patentability			
	Application number	Type	Description (minutes)	Claims (minutes)	Figures Analysis (minutes)	Total Step 1 (hours)	Formulation of the Search Strategy (minutes)	Execution of the Search Strategy (minutes)	Total Step 2 (hours)	Claims technical Analysis (minutes)	Prior Art Technical Analysis (minutes)	Comparison and Technical Justifications (minutes)	Total Step 3 (hours)
1						0			0				0
2						0			0				0
3						0			0				0
4						0			0				0
5						0			0				0
6						0			0				0
7						0			0				0
8						0			0				0
9						0			0				0
10						0			0				0

Figure 3.
Time for examination form.

i. If there are no more applications with any of the Classifications, repeat Steps 1 through 5 for the remaining Classifications until there are no more Applications available for distribution.

4.7 Final redistribution sample and calculation of the distribution balancing ratio (IBD)

In order to evaluate the distribution of the patent applications, a new data sample was obtained, referred to as Final Redistribution Sample. As the Standard Sample (with time) used to validate the model was obtained using examination data that, on their turn, were also based on international searches, this new redistribution sample was necessary to harmonize the examination process carried out by the examiners evaluated therein with the process implemented by the examiner, from which the Standard Sample with time was obtained. Based on this new sample, the proposed model and distribution logic are applied, and a Distribution Balancing Ratio (IBD) is then calculated, both for the original distribution and the new one, according to Eq. (12):

$$IBD = \frac{\sqrt{\sum_i \sum_j \left(\frac{m_{ed\,ij}}{M_{ed\,j}}\right)^2}}{\sqrt{\sum_i \sum_j \left(\frac{m_{ed\,ij}}{M_{ed\,j}}\right)^2 + \sum_i \sum_j \left(\frac{m_{ed\,ij} - M_{ed\,j}}{M_{ed\,j}}\right)^2}} \tag{12}$$

Where: m_{edij} is the median of variable j of patent applications distributed to examiner i; and M_{edj} is the median of variable j for all applications in the final redistribution sample.

In a first analysis of the IBD equation, it can be verified that the ratio seeks to capture and measure the influence of the differences between the medians of the variables of each examiner's samples and the general medians of the division's variables (complete sample). It is important to note that all medians of the variables composing the IBD are normalized (divided) by the general values of the respective medians of the complete sample. With that, we seek to avoid further distortions caused by different orders of magnitude of certain variables.

Additionally, as the several medians calculated can be higher or lower than the respective median of the division, the differences in these values can be positive or negative. Hence, as we wish to obtain an accumulated measurement of all differences in medians with no loss of information and without having a negative deviation in a certain variable compensating a positive deviation in another, we choose to square the differences and then add and extract the square root.

More specifically, when the numerator and the denominator of the IBD equation are analyzed, it can be noticed that both have the same first term, which is the sum of the squares of the normalized medians of all variables of interest from the examiners' samples. However, the denominator has a second additional term presenting the sum of the squares of the normalized differences between the medians of each examiner's individual samples and the medians of the corresponding variables from the complete sample.

It is important to highlight that, in an ideal distribution, the medians of the variables from all examiners' samples would be equal to the medians of the general variables of the division, i.e., the sum of the squares of the differences of the medians (second term of the IBD denominator) would be zero and, consequently, the IBD would be equal 1. On the other hand, a random distribution in which the examiners' samples have great differences in median values, when compared to the general division medians, would lead to very high denominator values, thus greatly reducing the IBD and, ultimately, making it tend to zero. Thereafter, we have that, the closer the medians of the variables from the examiners' individual samples are to the general medians of the division's variables, the greater and closer to 1 the IBD value will be and, consequently, better balanced the distribution will be.

5. Results

5.1 Determination of the examiners' ZAE and initial tests

Data were obtained from a total of eleven (11) Examiners from the Electricity Division, to be fully analyzed. For each patent application of such examiners with at least one examination already carried out, all variables of interest were obtained, totaling eight hundred and fourteen (814) patent applications to be evaluated and making up the initial test sample. Data from the Initial Test Sample were standardized according to Eq. (1). **Figure 4** shows the structure of data from the initial test sample with standardized data.

In the initial test sample, a total number of 95 main subclasses was found over all 814 patent applications analyzed. However, when considering only the examiners' ZAE (subclasses including 5% or more applications for each examiner), 25 main subclasses were responsible for 636 applications, i.e., about 80% of the total evaluated. It is important to highlight that, given that 3 of such 25 subclasses had very low occurrences, 22 subclasses were used in the set of interest for evaluation, equivalent to 619 applications (76% of total). **Figure 5** shows each one of the 11 examiners' areas of expertise by IPC subclasses. Note that the gray area corresponds to the examiners' Specific Areas of Expertise (ZAE), while the white area corresponds to

Order	Examiner	Application	Main Subclass	Pages of Description	Pages of Claims	Pages of Figures	Pages of Third Party Information	Independent Claims	Dependent Claims	Subclasses	Year of Filling	Inventors	Priorities
1	1	PI0101329-7	H01C	24	3	5	0	1	13	1	1	7	1
2	1	PI0111250-3	H01H	7	3	2	0	1	7	1	1	2	1
3	1	PI0400832-4	H02K	12	2	2	0	3	3	1	4	1	0
4	1	PI0403974-2	H01B	40	11	21	0	9	44	2	4	5	0
5	1	PI0107166-1	H01H	16	2	1	0	2	10	1	1	4	1
6	1	PI0303675-8	H02G	7	2	4	0	1	12	1	3	3	1
.	.	.	.	.	.	.	.	.	.	.	.	.	.
.	.	.	.	.	.	.	.	.	.	.	.	.	.
.	.	.	.	.	.	.	.	.	.	.	.	.	.
814	11	PI0601239-6	H05B	18	2	10	0	4	3	1	6	2	0

Figure 4.
Structure of the initial test sample with standardized data.

Examiners' Areas of Expertise by IPC Subclasses																					
1		2		3		4		5		6		7		8		9		10		11	
Subclass	%	Subclass	%	Subclass	%	Subclass	%	Subclass	%	Subclass	%	Subclass	%	Subclass	%	Subclass	%	Subclass	%	Subclass	%
H01H	63,08%	H01R	33,33%	H05B	18,42%	H02K	32,65%	H02J	19,54%	H02P	12,26%	H02K	56,36%	B66B	31,58%	G07F	17,09%	H01R	52,17%	B66B	12,09%
H02G	15,38%	H01H	23,33%	G01R	18,42%	H01M	14,29%	H02M	16,09%	B60L	9,43%	H01B	9,09%	B60T	14,04%	G08B	11,11%	H02G	24,64%	G01R	10,99%
H01B	6,15%	H01B	7,78%	H02P	15,79%	B60L	6,12%	G01R	13,79%	H02J	6,60%	H01R	7,27%	B60K	5,26%	B66B	7,69%	H02B	4,35%	H02B	8,79%
H01F	3,08%	G01R	6,67%	H01F	10,53%	G01R	4,08%	F02D	10,34%	F02D	6,60%	H01F	5,45%	F02D	5,26%	H05B	5,13%	H01H	2,90%	H01H	6,59%
H02K	1,54%	H05B	4,44%	H02H	7,89%	H02J	2,04%	B60K	4,60%	H01R	5,66%	F21V	3,64%	H02P	3,51%	F21V	5,13%	H02H	1,45%	H05B	4,40%
H02P	1,54%	H02H	3,33%	H01M	7,89%	F21V	2,04%	H02H	4,60%	B60K	3,77%	G01R	1,82%	H02G	1,75%	G01R	3,42%	H02K	1,45%	F21V	3,30%
H02B	1,54%	H02J	3,33%	H01H	5,26%	H02H	2,04%	H01M	4,60%	H02K	3,77%	H02G	1,82%	H02H	1,75%	H02H	2,56%			B60L	2,20%
		H02K	2,22%	H02G	2,63%	H02P	2,04%	H02G	1,15%	H01F	3,77%	H02B	1,82%			H01H	2,56%			H01R	1,10%
		H02G	2,22%	B60K	2,63%	H01H	2,04%	H01F	1,15%	H01M	3,77%	H01M	1,82%			H02J	1,71%			H01M	1,10%
				H02K	2,63%	H02B	2,04%	B60L	1,15%	H05B	3,77%					H01M	1,71%			H02J	1,10%
						H02G	2,04%	H01H	1,15%	H02H	2,83%					H02K	0,85%			H02H	1,10%
								H02P	1,15%	G01R	1,89%					H01F	0,85%			B60T	1,10%
										F21V	0,94%					B60L	0,85%			H02P	1,10%
										H01H	0,94%										

Figure 5.
Examiners' areas of expertise by IPC subclass.

subclasses that, despite not being part of the examiner's ZAE, are part of the ZAE of some of the other examiners evaluated.

Figures 6 and 7 show the results obtained in the PCA.

By analyzing **Figure 6**, when using only the criterion considering eigenvalues higher than one, only the first four (4) components would be selected. However, these would be responsible for about 65% of total variance. It can also be verified that the range sharply drops when we get to the eigenvalue of component 6 (0.73). Additionally, the first five components explain a total variance of 75.05%. Hence, these first five components were selected for the next steps.

In **Figure** 7, the significant factors to each variable (very close to or above 0.4) were hatched in gray. In a first analysis, it can be noticed that component Y1 is quite detached from the others. In addition to explaining virtually 30% of all variance, the component is associated with variables directly related to the volume of data (pages of description, of claims, and of figures, in addition to the number of independent and dependent claims). Such fact is consistent with the initial hypothesis 1, related to the volume variables. As for components Y2 and Y3, although they may be slightly related to the volume of data, they basically represent the influences of variables, year of filing, number of inventors, and priorities. These components appear to be associated with development strategies, management of the applicants, and maturity of the technology involved. On the other hand, components Y4 and Y5

Principal Component	Eigenvalues	Variance	Accumulated variance
Y1	2,95	29,53%	29,53%
Y2	1,48	14,82%	44,36%
Y3	1,12	11,18%	55,53%
Y4	1,03	10,29%	65,82%
Y5	0,92	9,23%	75,05%
Y6	0,73	7,33%	82,39%
Y7	0,71	7,12%	89,51%
Y8	0,53	5,25%	94,77%
Y9	0,34	3,43%	98,19%
Y10	0,18	1,81%	100,00%

Figure 6.
Eigenvalues and variances.

Variable	Weighting Coefficients (Scores)				
	Y1	Y2	Y3	Y4	Y5
Pages of Description	0,4143	-0,316	-0,1136	-0,0525	0,0835
Pages of Claims	0,4978	0,1897	0,2442	-0,0058	-0,0719
Pages of Figures	0,3317	-0,487	-0,2236	-0,1627	-0,0517
Pages of Third Party Info	-0,0594	-0,0591	0,3375	-0,6677	0,6526
Independent Claims	0,3932	0,2189	0,2599	0,0367	-0,0534
Dependent Claims	0,4574	0,25	0,2467	-0,0404	-0,1294
Subclassess	0,0322	-0,201	0,3019	0,7121	0,5457
Year of Filling	-0,0876	-0,456	0,5003	0,0443	-0,2269
Inventors	0,2168	-0,4437	-0,2729	-0,0036	0,0224
Priorities	0,218	0,2606	-0,4682	0,1138	0,4359

Figure 7.
Weighting coefficients.

complement the others by being associated with the variables, number of sub-classes, and pages of third party observations. Such components appear to represent specific influences of the technological area of the patent applications. This result is consistent with the initial hypothesis 2, related to the variables with complementary or indirect influences.

By applying the proposed redistribution logic, a new configuration of samples by examiner was obtained. **Figure 8** shows a comparison between the percentage of applications distributed to each examiner within their ZAE.

By analyzing **Figure 8**, it is possible to note that, for ten out of the eleven examiners, there was a significant increase in the number of applications distributed to them and pertaining to their own ZAE. Only examiner 9 had a small decrease (that could even be corrected with a fine adjustment), due to the fact that his data sample was significantly larger than that of the others. Thus, this new configuration seems to contribute to examiners to work within their specific fields of expertise and knowledge.

Finally, the IBD ratios of the original sample distribution and its redistribution were calculated. Through Eq. (12), an IBD equal to 0.86 for the original case and an IBD equal to 0.88 for the redistribution were obtained, i.e., there was an increase in the IBD with the new distribution, evidencing that the medians of the examiners' applications after redistribution are closer to the general division's median. Such fact corroborates the fact that with the new distribution, we have a tendency towards greater balance regarding volume of data/complexity of applications distributed to the examiners.

5.2 Model validation: simulations using standard sample with time

Similarly to the procedure carried out for the initial test sample, data of patent applications of the technological area regarding electrical engineering were obtained. However, as, in this case, we intend to obtain a standard sample with time to serve as a reference, all data were obtained from the time for examination form filled by a single examiner. For each patent application of such examiner, all variables of interest were obtained, for a total amount of fifty (50) patent applications, with all first actions already published. Data were collected between January and July 2020, with all sample applications using data from previous searches by international offices.

We note that from the ten possible variables to be analyzed, the only one that was not considered in this case was the number of pages of third parties observations, given that there is no application with such document available in the sample.

For the sensitivity analysis of the model, dozens of simulations were performed considering all cases: from the most complete one, with nine variables, to the simplest ones, with three variables. For all cases, simulations for each ten sample applications were performed, i.e., for each set of cases with three to nine variables, tests were performed considering 10, 20, 30, 40, and 50 patent applications of the standard sample. A minimum of ten test applications was chosen, as it is recommended that the sample should have a population at least larger than the

Examiner	1	2	3	4	5	6	7	8	9	10	11
New ZAE	90,63%	76,14%	97,37%	87,50%	85,06%	46,73%	83,64%	81,03%	41,88%	91,30%	76,92%
Original ZAE	84,62%	71,11%	84,21%	53,06%	59,77%	40,57%	78,18%	56,14%	46,15%	76,81%	38,46%

Figure 8.
Percentage of applications within the ZAE before and after the new distribution.

number of variables in order to apply the PCA method, provided that the larger the sample, in theory, the best for the model.

When executing the simulations, the correlations of all variables and of the IGC ratios with time were verified, and the IGC was calculated both using the criterion of 70% of the variance, being referred to as $IGC_{70\%}$, and using the criterion of eigenvalues higher than one, being referred to as $IGC_{\lambda>1}$. It is important to note that, when $IGC_{70\%}$ and $IGC_{\lambda>1}$ are equal, we will refer to it simply as IGC. Finally, an IGC related only to the principal component (Y1) of the cases, the most significant component in terms of variance, being referred to as IGC_{Y1}, was also calculated.

After executing all the simulations, and having a gamut of results for dozens of cases, the cases of more relevance and interest in terms of analyzed variables and their correlations with time were selected. Namely:

- Case 1– Case 9 Var, complete with the nine variables;
- Case 2 – Case 5 Var, including only the five variables of direct volume;
- Case 3 – Case 4 Var, similar to case 2, but excluding the variable "number of pages of figures" (given that this variable presented lower scores in the PCA and the lowest individual correlation with time among the five of volume);
- Case 4 – Case 3 Var, similar to case 3, but aggregating the amount of dependent and independent claims in only one variable (i.e., considering pages of description, claim pages, and total claims); and
- Case 5 – Case 3 Var (2), similar to case 4, but replacing the pages of description with the total of pages. Hence, the following variables were considered: total number of pages, claim pages and total claims.

Figures 9 and **10** show the results of eigenvalues and cumulative variances for all the five described Cases.

By analyzing **Figures 9** and **10**, it is possible to note that:

- Case 9 Var: simulations using 10 and 20 applications deviate from the others, and the cases using 30 to 50 applications are almost coincident, i.e., the

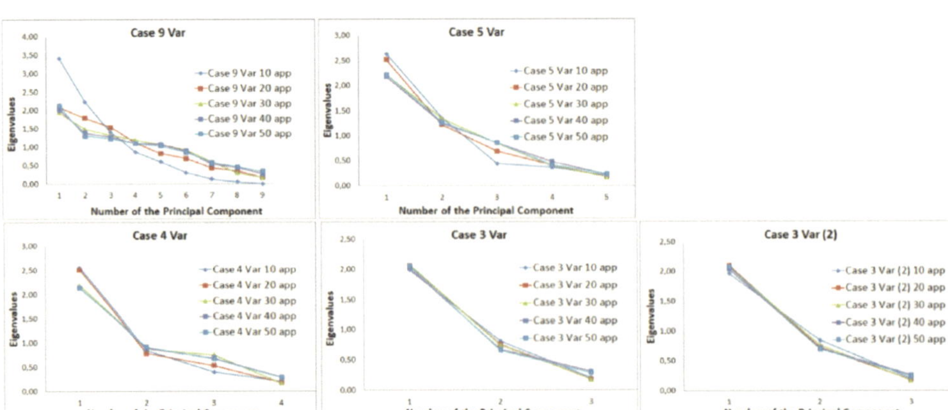

Figure 9.
Eigenvalues of cases 1 to 5.

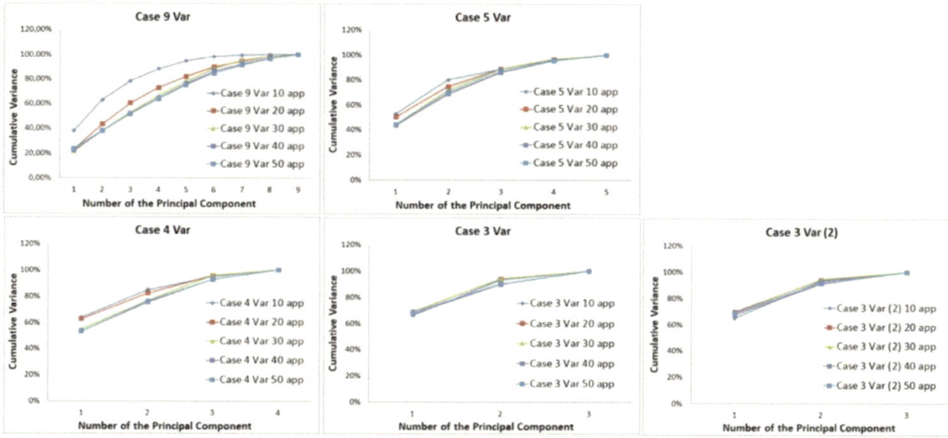

Figure 10.
Cumulative variances of cases 1 to 5.

eigenvalues of the components only tend to be stable starting in the sample with 30 applications. The same phenomenon can be observed by analyzing the cumulative variances of the samples. These results evidence that, for cases with nine variables that are intended to be executed, a sample of at least 30 patent applications, preferably 50 applications, is recommended to obtain better performance of the PCA method;

- Case 5 Var: only the simulation using a sample of 10 applications quite deviates from the others; the case using 20 applications shows a slight deviation; and cases using 30 to 50 applications are almost coincident, i.e., the eigenvalues of the components already tend to be stable starting in the sample with 20 applications. The same phenomenon can be observed by analyzing the cumulative variances of the samples. These results evidence that, for cases with five variables that are intended to be executed, a sample of at least 20 patent applications, preferably 30 applications, is recommended to obtain better performance of the PCA method;

- Case 4 Var: simulations using 10 and 20 applications slightly deviate from the others, and the cases using 30 to 50 applications are coincident, i.e., the eigenvalues of the components already tend to be quite stable starting in the sample with 10 applications, and very stable starting in 30 applications. The same phenomenon can be observed by analyzing the cumulative variances of the samples. These results evidence that, for cases with four variables that are intended to be executed, a sample of at least 10 patent applications, preferably 20 applications, is recommended to obtain better performance of the PCA method.

- Case 3 Var and Case 3 Var(2): all simulations, from samples of 10 to 50 applications, are virtually coincident, i.e., the eigenvalues of the components have excellent stability. The same phenomenon can be observed by analyzing the cumulative variances of the samples. These results evidence that, for cases with three variables that are intended to be executed, a sample of at least 10 patent applications, preferably 20 applications, is recommended to obtain better performance of the PCA method.

Figures 11 and **12** show the results of correlations of the IGC with time.

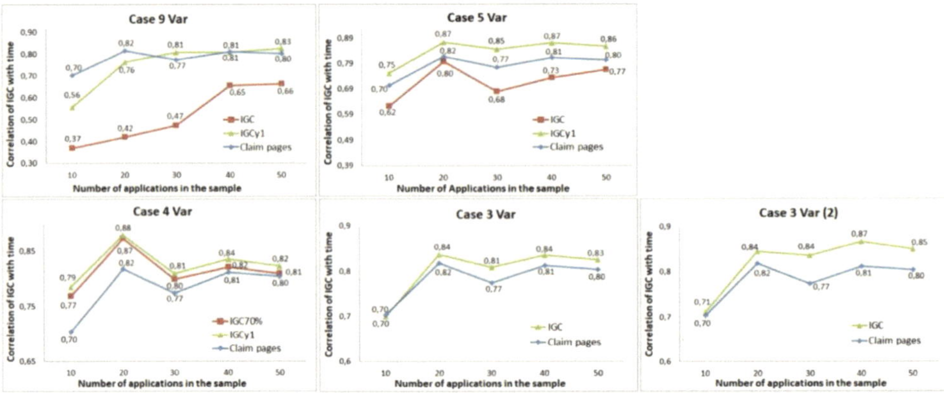

Figure 11.
Correlation of the IGC with the time for examination – cases 1 to 5.

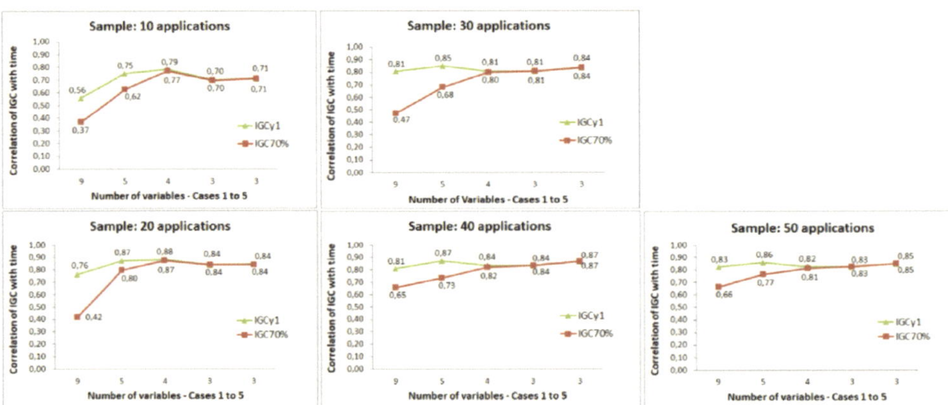

Figure 12.
Correlation of the IGC with the time for examination – cases 1 to 5 – By samples.

The analysis of **Figures 11** and **12** indicates that:

- Case 9 Var: based on a sample with a total of 30 patent applications, there is a slight advantage of correlation with time for IGC_{Y1}, and both are very close to the value of 0.8;

- Case 5 Var: except for the sample with 20 applications, the larger the sample, the greater the correlation of the IGC with time. On the other hand, upon analysis of the IGC_{Y1}, that is, considering only the most significant principal component, basically related to the main direct volume variables, the correlation with time increases significantly, reaching even larger values (0.86). It is also worth to highlight that the correlation of the IGC_{Y1} with time increases a lot when the sample have 20 applications instead of 10; from then on, it seems to stabilize, oscillating around 0.85. This result proves to be consistent with the profile of the eigenvalues and cumulative variances analyzed, reinforcing the need for a sample with a least 20 applications. Finally, a very similar profile is noted in the three curves. Once again, the IGC_{Y1} has better results upon analysis of the correlation with time;

- Case 4 Var: the profile of the three curves is quite similar, and, based on the sample with 30 applications, the correlation with time of all ratios gets close to

0.80 and oscillates around that. It is also worth to highlight that both IGC curves show a good correlation with time even based on a sample with only 10 applications, a result that proves to be consistent with the profile of the eigenvalues and cumulative variances analyzed. Finally, it can be noticed that, although the correlation values of the three curves are close to each other, once again, the IGC_{Y1} (in this case also equal to the $IGC_{\lambda>1}$) has an advantage over the others;

- Case 3 Var: the profile of both curves is quite similar, and, based on the sample with 20 applications, the correlation with time of all ratios gets close to 0.80 and oscillates around that. It is also worth to highlight that both curves already show a reasonable correlation with time even based on a sample with only 10 applications, a result that proves to be consistent with the profile of the eigenvalues and cumulative variances analyzed. Finally, it can be noticed that, although the correlation values of both curves are close to each other, once again, the IGC (in this case $IGC = IGC_{70\%} = IGC_{\lambda>1} = IGC_{Y1}$) has an advantage.

- Case 3 Var (2): based on the sample with 20 applications, the correlation of the IGC with time is always above 0.84. It is also worth to highlight that both curves already show a reasonable correlation with time even based on a sample with only 10 applications, a result that proves to be consistent with the profile of the eigenvalues and cumulative variances. Finally, it can be noticed that this is the case in which the IGC (once again, $IGC = IGC_{70\%} = IGC_{\lambda>1} = IGC_{Y1}$) has the higher values of correlation with time, so it has an advantage regarding all variables individually. In addition to having a high correlation with time, this is the most indicated case for practical application, because, besides having only three variables and principal components with great stability, it does not require a division of the claims into independent and dependent, which greatly facilitates the data collection.

The analysis of **Figures 11** and **12** also indicates that the profile of the curves is quite similar, with an increasing trend for the correlation of the IGC with time in the beginning of all of them, i.e., when the number of variables decreases from nine to five, and, from five to three variables, the curves stabilize. These results reflect the previous analyses that showed that, when only the direct volume variables are selected (with their combinations varying), the trend was for obtaining higher and more stable correlations with time. Thus, although all nine variables of the study may contribute to the complexity of the patent application, in practice, the direct volume variables already represent well the examination effort/time.

It should also be noted that the correlations of the IGC_{Y1} with time remained high and almost constant for any of the cases analyzed with samples with twenty applications or more, showing a quite stable behavior regardless of the sample size. Consequently, for the problem in particular, the results converge showing that the IGC_{Y1} ratio seems more suitable to represent the examination effort/time. The results obtained suggest that Case 3 Var (2) is the one with the best cost–benefit relation for the performance of even more specific practical tests, whether because it captures the influences of the main variables of direct volume data, because it is simpler regarding obtaining and collecting data (as it does not require a division of the claims into independent and dependent), or because it has higher correlations of the IGC with time.

Figure 13 shows the classifications of the Sample applications by time and by the IGC_{Y1}. **Table 1** shows the applications in which there was divergence in the classification.

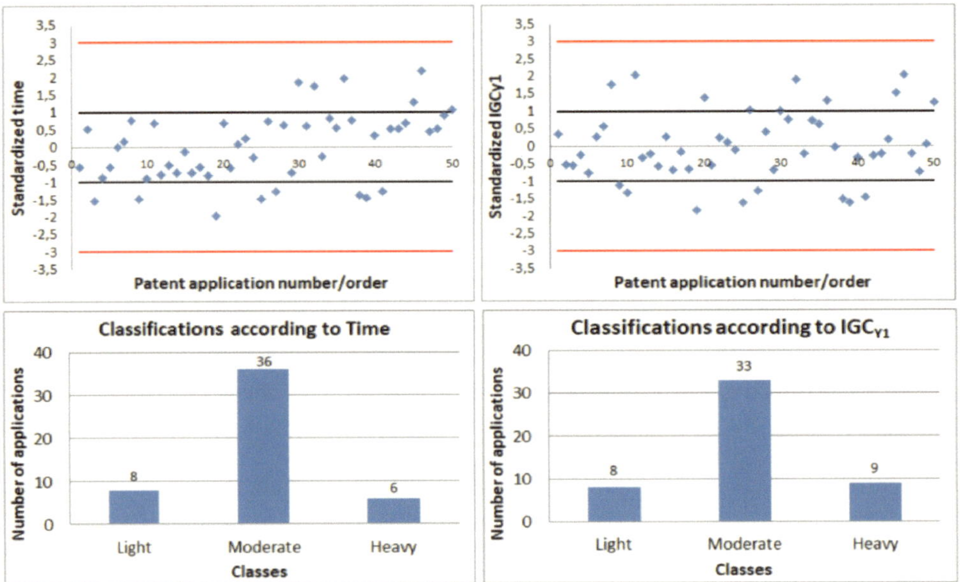

Figure 13.
Classification of applications of the standard sample (with time).

Comparison of Classifications according to Time and IGC_{Y1}					
Application	**Claim Pages**	**Total Pages**	**Total Claims**	**Classification according to the Time**	**Classification according to IGC_{Y1}**
3	2	34	5	Light	Moderate
8	5	50	15	Moderate	Heavy
10	2	13	3	Moderate	Light
11	6	37	19	Moderate	Heavy
20	5	34	16	Moderate	Heavy
26	4	36	15	Moderate	Heavy
30	4	56	8	Heavy	Moderate

Table 1.
Applications with divergent classifications.

By analyzing **Figure 13**, it can be verified that, when classified by time for examination, none of the applications from the sample was considered to be neither very light nor very heavy. Most applications were classified as moderate (36 or 72%), then light (8 or 16%), followed by heavy (6 or 12%). This result proves to be consistent with data obtained, as the standard sample is fairly homogeneous, shows applications of the same type of examination (using data from previous searches), and the time variable presented a moderate coefficient of variation (16.58%). Similarly to the classification by time, when classified by the IGC_{Y1}, none of the patent applications from the sample was considered to be neither very light nor very heavy. Most applications were classified as moderate (33 or 66%), then heavy (9 or 18%), followed by light (8 or 16%).

By analyzing **Table 1**, it can be verified that there was a total of seven patent applications with conflicting classifications by time and IGC_{Y1}. Therefore, this result shows that the classification of 43 of the 50 applications (86% of the total) converged, in other words, it shows great similarity. It is important to note that the correlation of the IGC_{Y1} with time for the case under analysis was 0.85, i.e., the classification criterion proved to be efficient, managing to keep up with the capture tendency of this relation of the ratio with the time. More specifically to the differences found, there were four new classifications according to the IGC_{Y1} as heavy (applications 8, 11, 20, and 26). Such applications have higher than average number of claim pages, total number of pages, and total number of claims, showing a profile similar to the other five heavy applications with similar classifications and, so, its classification as heavy according to the IGC_{Y1} is warranted. On the other hand, it can be noticed that applications 20 and 26 showed IGC values close to one, i.e., to the classification limit between the moderate and heavy ranges. Consequently, there are two factors that may possibly explain this phenomenon: i) errors inherent in the mathematical model, which, although in small amounts, tend to occur depending on the variables, samples, and criteria adopted; and ii) measurement errors or deviations in time, which could move a classification close to the limit of the ranges.

Regarding application 10, classified as light according to the IGC_{Y1} and as moderate according to time, it is possible to note it is indeed a quite short application that, at first, would actually tend to be classified as light. Specifically in this case, the standardized time was very near to minus one (standardized time = − 0.91), i.e., quite near to the limit between moderate and light classes. Unlike the conflicting heavy cases (in which deviations probably occurred for reasons inherent in the model), in this case the tendency is that time measurement deviations may have caused the discrepancy.

In the case of application 3, classified as moderate according to the IGC_{Y1} and as light according to time, we notice that it is an application with few claims and few claim pages, but with a quite high count of total pages. Depending on the specific examination procedure and the need to better understand the description and the figures, time may lead to a moderate or light classification. Hence, it is a type of application difficult to classify *a priori* and, in this case, the model was more conservative, classifying it as moderate.

Finally, application number thirty, classified as moderate according to the IGC_{Y1} and heavy according to time, showed a IGC_{Y1} virtually equal to one ($IGC_{Y1} = 0.995$), reaching the exact limit between the moderate and heavy classification ranges. It ends up being a case similar to the discrepancies of the heavy applications, due to issues inherent in the mathematical model.

In short, it can be verified that the model manages to represent quite satisfactorily the examination time/effort, and for cases in the threshold of the criteria adopted, few discrepancies occur, and, in these cases, the discrepancies occur only in the adjacent ranges. In other words, any discrepancies that occur are occasional, not rough, and reasonable given the limitations inherent in this kind of model and research.

5.3 Analysis of the redistribution logic: simulations with the final redistribution sample

Ten patent applications of ten examiners under analysis were selected to compose the final redistribution sample, amounting to one hundred (100) patent applications to be examined. The steps of the proposed methodology were strictly followed, but, due to the fact that the purpose of this case was to obtain a sample to apply the model validated with the standard sample with time (our reference), all variables of interest were obtained of first examinations already published, collected between May and July 2020, and all sample applications are also using data from previous searches by international offices (in the context of the "backlog

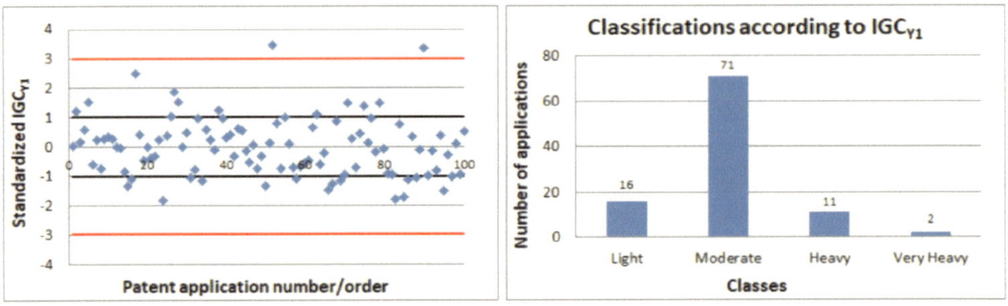

Figure 14.
classifications of the Redistribution sample applications.

Examiner	1	2	3	4	5	6	7	8	9	10
New ZAE	70,00%	50,00%	40,00%	60,00%	40,00%	50,00%	30,00%	10,00%	90,00%	40,00%
Original ZAE	80,00%	50,00%	40,00%	40,00%	10,00%	0,00%	20,00%	10,00%	30,00%	0,00%

Figure 15.
Percentage of applications within the ZAE before and after the new distribution.

combat plan", i.e., without executing specific prior art search). The case chosen for the redistribution simulation was Case 5 – Case 3 Var (2), given that this case obtained the best results in the validation tests with the standard sample with time. **Figure 14** shows the classifications of the redistribution sample applications.

None of the sample patent applications were classified as very light. Most applications were classified as moderate (71%), followed by light (16%), heavy (11%), and, finally, very heavy, which were only two (2%). It should be noted that the data on the IGC_{Y1} showed normal statistical distribution, similarly to the time and the IGC_{Y1} of the standard sample.

Figure 15 indicates that with the redistribution there was a better balance in the concentration of applications within the ZAE of each examiner. We note that in the case of six out of the ten examiners, there was an increased number of applications distributed to them and pertaining to their own ZAE, with an emphasis on examiners 5, 6, 9 and 10, with significant increases. Only examiner 8 remained with a poor concentration (10%) of applications within his ZAE, which may be explained by the fact that this examiner is a more "versatile" examiner of the division, and does not have such a well defined ZAE. Thus, the results suggest that this new configuration contributes for the examiners to work within their specific fields of expertise and knowledge.

To complement the cycle of the methodology and make a last comparison between the distributions, the IBD ratios of the original sample distribution and of its redistribution were calculated. Eq. (12) resulted in an IBD equal to 0.83 for the original case and an IBD equal to 0.9 for the redistribution, i.e., there was an increased IBD with the new distribution, showing that the medians of the applications of the examiners after redistribution get closer to the general median of the division. This corroborates the fact that the new distribution results in a trend for better balance regarding the volume of data and time/effort of the applications distributed to the examiners.

6. Final considerations

In this study, ten possible variables were identified, relevant to the evaluation and distribution of the patent applications to the examiners. Among these variables, the ones directly related to the voluminosity of a patent document, i.e., the volume of data that the examiner has to deal with when examining patents, were identified, namely: the number of pages of description, the number of claim pages, the number of pages of figures, the number of independent claims and the number of dependent claims.

With the application of the PCA in a first data sample, referred to as Initial Test Sample, it was verified that the components were consistent with the initial hypotheses. Based on this initial sample, containing a large number of applications examined over two years, the examiners' Specific Areas of Expertise (ZAE) were determined, that is, the IPC subclasses (technological areas) they examine the most according to their knowledge and work experience. These ZAE are highly relevant, as these subclasses are one of the criteria used to distribute patent applications to the examiners, and their comparison before and after any redistribution is important.

The patent applications were also classified in up to five classes: very light, light, moderate, heavy, and very heavy, and the classification had as a reference the IGC values, considering ranges equivalent to the average ratio plus one, three or more standard deviations. Then the applications were redistributed with emphasis on the examiners' ZAE and on the classifications. The results show that the medians of the examiners' applications approached the general medians of the division, suggesting that the new distribution is more balanced in volume of data than the original one. Moreover, with the new distribution, the examiners had the majority of their applications allocated within their respective ZAE, i.e., they would examine more applications in their specific areas of knowledge and preference, also suggesting that the new distribution contributes to better efficiency, quality, and motivation.

Additionally, the results obtained suggest that, although the five variables directly related to volume of data tend to be the ones that mostly impact the examination process, all ten variables selected, to some extent, influence the analysis of complexity of patent applications.

On the other hand, as complexity is something relative, to investigate if this complexity indeed captures the examination time/effort, a sensitivity analysis of the model developed was performed in order to verify the correlations of variables and IGC with time. In order to do so, it was then necessary to obtain a new sample of patent applications, referred to as Standard Sample, now with the additional collection of the examination time variable. In this context, simulations considering different variables and standard sample sizes were performed, with application of the PCA method and the model developed, including calculation of the IGC with different criteria and their correlations with time. The results obtained suggest that, for our specific problem, the IGC with greater efficiency and stability was IGC_{Y1}, i.e., using only the first principal component, the one which is most representative as to total data variance.

It is also worth noting that the case including only three variables (number of claim pages, total number of pages, and total number of claims) is the one recommended to perform even more specific practical tests, whether because it captures the influences of the main variables of direct volume of data, given the simplicity for data acquisition and collection (as it does not require separation of independent claims from the dependent ones), or because it has consistently higher correlations of the IGC_{Y1} with time, always close to 0.85.

Based on this new sample with the collection of the time for examination, the patent applications were once again classified into the five classes defined (very light, light, moderate, heavy and very heavy). Such classifications were carried out twice, the first time using the time for examination variable as a reference, i.e., the standard reference classification, and the second time using the IGC_{Y1} ratio, i.e., the classification suggested by the model. Upon comparison between these classifications according to time and the classifications of the model, the results showed a strong similarity, as the model correctly classified 43 out of the 50 patent applications analyzed, a total of 86%.

After testing the mathematical model and the criteria for classification with the correlations with time, the following step was to perform a first practical complete redistribution test. In order to do so, it was necessary to collect a third and final sample, referred to as Final Redistribution Sample, with 100 patent applications, being 10 applications of 10 different examiners, all using data from previous searches by international offices, so that the profile of this new sample was similar to the profile of the standard sample, as our reference had already been tested. Based on this new sample, we determined the main central tendency statistics of the samples by examiner and calculated the Distribution Balancing Ratios (IBD) both for the original distribution and for the sample redistributed according to the IGC_{Y1}.

The results obtained with the new redistribution showed that there was a better balance in the examination concentration within the ZAE of each examiner, and in the samples of six out of the ten examiners analyzed, there was an increased number of applications distributed to them and pertaining to their own ZAE. Thus, there is evidence that this new configuration contributes for the examiners to work within their specific fields of expertise and knowledge and, consequently, to their efficiency and motivation. It should also be noted that the new redistribution produced a positive effect on the medians of the examiners' samples, which was mathematically quantified by calculating the IBD, which, in the original distribution, had a value of 0.83 and, after redistribution, increased to 0.90.

In short, our results suggest that the mathematical model is able to represent quite satisfactorily the examination time/effort for patent applications. Also, the logic proposed managed to achieve the goal of better balancing the examiners' workload distribution.

Author details

Cesar Vianna Moreira Júnior[1]*, Daniel Marques Golodne[2] and Ricardo Carvalho Rodrigues[1]

1 Brazilian National Institute of Industrial Property (Intellectual Property Academy), Rio de Janeiro, Brazil

2 Brazilian National Institute of Industrial Property (Patent Office—DIRPA), Rio de Janeiro, Brazil

*Address all correspondence to: cvmjunior@gmail.com

IntechOpen

© 2021 The Author(s). Licensee IntechOpen. This chapter is distributed under the terms of the Creative Commons Attribution License (http://creativecommons.org/licenses/by/3.0), which permits unrestricted use, distribution, and reproduction in any medium, provided the original work is properly cited.

References

[1] INPI. Plano de Combate ao Backlog. Available at: https://www.gov.br/inpi/pt-br/servicos/patentes/plano-de-combate-ao-backlog. [Retrived on: 2019-08-13].

[2] INPI. Novo INPI: Protocolo de Madri e Plano de Combate ao Backlog de Patentes. Available at: http://www.inpi.gov.br/noticias/protocolo-de-madri-e-plano-de-combate-ao-backlog-de-patentes/ [Retrived on: 2020-03-02].

[3] INPI. INPI tem novo Plano Estratégico com missão e visão 2021. Available at: http://www.inpi.gov.br/noticias/inpi-tem-novo-plano-estrategico-com-missao-e-visao-2021/ [Retrived on: 2020-03-02].

[4] INPI. INPI e EPO lançam parceria técnica e estratégica na área de patentes. Available at: http://www.inpi.gov.br/noticias/inpi-e-epo-lancam-parceria-tecnica-e-estrategica-na-area-de-patentes/ [Retrived on: 2020-03-03].

[5] De Saint-Georges, M. & de la Potterie, B. V. P. A quality index for patent systems; Research Policy, 42(3), p. 704-719. 2013.

[6] Philipp, M. Patent filing and searching: Is deflation in quality the inevitable consequence of hyperinflation in quantity? World Patent Information, 28(2), p. 117-121. 2006.

[7] Kim, Y. K., & Oh, J. B. Examination workloads, grant decision bias and examination quality of patent office. Research Policy, 46(5), p. 1005-1019, 2017.

[8] Golodne, D. M., & Silva, A. S. Managing patent examiners' workload by using patent application volume data. *Manuscript submitted for publication*, June, 2020.

[9] BRAZIL. Law No. 9,279 of May 14, 1996 [Brazilian Industrial Property Law]. Regulating rights and obligations related to industrial property. Available at: http://www.planalto.gov.br/ccivil_03/leis/L9279.htm [Retrived on: 2017-02-01].

[10] INPI. INPI Normative Instruction No. 30 of 2013.

[11] Soares, P. L. L., Moreira Jr., C. V., Rodrigues, R. C. & Braga, E. J. O Papel do Termo Caracterizante nos Documentos de Patentes na Delimitação de Direitos em Propriedade Industrial. Revista da ABPI – n° 161 – Jul/Ago 2019, p. 26-40. 2019.

[12] Oliveira, L. G., Suster, R., Pinto, A. C., Ribeiro, N. M. & Silva, R. B. Informação em Patentes: Ferramenta Indispensável para a Pesquisa e o Desenvolvimento Tecnológico. Química Nova, Vol. 28, S36-S40. 2005.

[13] ORGANIZAÇÃO MUNDIAL DA PROPRIEDADE INTELECTUAL – OMPI. Norma ST.9 - Manual de Informação e Documentação em Matéria de Propriedade Industrial. 2013. Available at: https://www.wipo.int/export/sites/www/standards/es/pdf/03-09-01.pdf [Retrived on: 2019-11-01].

[14] WORLD INTELLECTUAL PROPERTY ORGANIZATION – WIPO. International Patent Classification (IPC). Available at: https://www.wipo.int/classifications/ipc/ipcpub [Retrived on: 2019-11-01].

[15] Delvizio, E. Avaliação das estratégias da indústria para-petrolífera pelos respectivos depósitos de patentes. In: Rio Oil & Gas Expo and Conference 2010; Rio de Janeiro; 2010.

[16] Harloff, D. & Wagner, S. Modeling the Duration of Patent Examination at European Patent Office. GESY; Discussion Paper 170; 2006.

[17] Gambardella, A., Harhoff, D. & Verspagen, B. The Value of European Patents. European Management Review, 5(2), p. 69-84. 2008.

[18] Kuhn, J. M. & Thompson, N.C. How to Measure and Draw Causal Inferences with Patent Scope. Working Paper. 2017.

[19] Marco, A. C., Sarnoff, J. D. & de Grazia, C. Patent Claims and Patent Scope. Working paper. 2016.

[20] Cocknurn, I. M., Kortum, S. & Stern, S. Are All Patent Examiners Equal? The Impact of Examiner Characteristics. NBER Working Paper 8980. 2002.

[21] Lemley, M. A. & Sampat, B. Examiner Chacacteristics and Patent Office Outcomes. Review of Economics and Statistics 94(3), p. 817-827. 2012.

[22] Cesare, R. & Timothy, S. Patent Examiner Specialization. NBER Working Paper. 2018.

[23] Archontopoulos, E., Guellec, D., Stevnsborg, N., de la Potterie, B. V. P. & Zeebroeck, N. V. When small is beautiful: Measuring the evolution and consequences of the voluminosity of patent applications at the EPO. Information Economics and Policy, 19 (2), p. 103-132. 2007.

[24] Van Zeebroeck, N., Stevnsborg, N., de la Potterie, B. V. P., Guellec, D., & Archontopoulos, E. Patent inflation in Europe. World Patent Information, 30 (1), p. 43-52. 2008.

[25] Van Zeebroeck, N., de la Potterie, B. V. P. & Guellec, D. Claiming more: the increased voluminosity of patent applications and its determinants. Research Policy, 38(6), p. 1006-1020. 2009.

[26] Johnson, R. A., Wichern, D. W. Applied Multivariate Statistical Analysis, New Jersey: Prentice-Hall, Inc., 5 ed., 797p. 2002.

[27] Rencher, A. C. Methods of Multivariate Analysis. John Wiley and Sons, 2 ed., 740p. 2002.

[28] Paiva, A. P. Metodologia de Superfície de Resposta e Análise de Componentes Principais em Otimização de Processos de Manufatura com Múltiplas Respostas Correlacionadas. Tese (Doutorado) – Universidade Federal de Itajubá, Instituto de Engenharia Mecânica, 257p. 2006.

[29] Herig, L. C. T. O Modelo das Componentes Principais: apresentação e interpretações. Tese (mestrado) – Universidade Federal do Rio de Janeiro, Faculdade de Engenharia. 222p. 1979.

[30] Vicini, Lorena. Análise multivariada da teoria à prática. Monografia (Especialização) – Universidade Federal de Santa Maria, Faculdade de Estatística. 215p. 2005.

[31] Hongyu, K., Sandanielo, V. L. M., Junior, G. J. de O. Análise de componentes principais: resumo teórico, aplicação e interpretação. Engineering and Science, V.1, 5ed. 2015.

[32] Meira, C. T.; Pereira, I. G.; Farah, M. M.; Pires, A. V.; Garcia, D. A.; Cruz, V. A. R. Seleção de características morfofuncionais de cavalos da raça Manga larga Marchador por meio da análise decomponentes principais. Arquivo Brasileiro de Medicina Veterinária e Zootecnia, 65, p. 1843–1848. 2013.

[33] Paiva, A.L.C.; Teixeira, R.B.; Yamaki, M.; Menezes, G.R.O.; Leite, C. . S.; Torres, R.A. Análise de componentes principais em características de produção de aves de postura. Revista Brasileira de Zootecnia, 39, p. 285–288. 2010.

[34] Savenago, R.P., Caetano, S.L., Ramos, S.B., Nascimento, G.B.,

Schmidt, G.S., Ledur, M.C. Munari, D.P. Estimates ofgenetic parameters, and cluster and principal components analysesof breeding values related to egg production traits in a White Leghorn population. Poultry Science, 90, p.2174-2188. 2011.

[35] Silva, M. C., Silva, J. D. G., Borges, E. F. Análises de componentes principais para elaborar índices de desempenho no setor público. Revista Brasileira de Biomedicina, v.33, n.3, p.291-309. 2015.

[36] Begnini, S., Almeida, L. E. D. F. Grau de desenvolvimento dos municípios da mesorregião oeste catarinense: caracterização e classificação. Revista Interações, v.17, n.4, p.547-560. 2016.

[37] Hongyu, K. Comparação do GGE-biplot ponderado e AMMI-ponderado com outros modelos de interação genótipo × ambiente. Tese (Doutorado em Estatística e Experimentação Agronômica) - Escola Superior de Agricultura "Luiz de Queiroz", Universidade de São Paulo, Piracicaba. 155p. 2015.

[38] Kaiser, H. F. The varimax criterion for analytic rotation in fator analysis. Psychometrika, v. 23, n. 3.p. 187-200. 1958.

[39] Cattel, R. B. The Screen Test for the Number of Factors. Multivariate Behavior Research, V. 1, p. 245-276. 1966.

[40] Scremin, M. A. A. Método para Seleção do Número de Componentes Principais com base na Lógica difusa. Tese de Doutorado em Engenharia de Produção, Universidade Federal de Santa Cataria, 124p. 2003.

[41] Sandanielo, V. L. M. Emprego de técnicas estatísticas na construção de índices de desenvolvimento sustentável aplicados a assentamentos rurais. Tese (doutorado) - Universidade Estadual Paulista, Faculdade de Ciências Agronômicas de Botucatu, 159p. 2008.

Chapter 6

Comparative Analysis of Appeal Procedures in the European, American and Brazilian Patent Offices

Fabio Monteiro dos Santos, Heleno José Costa Bezerra Netto and Ricardo Carvalho Rodrigues

Abstract

The right to appeal exists as a response to the two main characteristics of every human being. The first refers to the attitude of not settling for adverse decisions, which leads people to seek instruments to remediate these decisions, while the second is the possibility that every human being has to make mistakes and the need to correct these mistakes in decision-making acts that may have been mistaken. Therefore, an appeal is an instrument that enables review of a decision by a higher authority to obtain its modification or revocation. In the patent system, appeals are used basically to reverse decisions of patent examiners during the examination procedure as, for example, the decision to reject a patent. Although all patent offices have procedures for appeal against first-instance decisions taken by these offices, there are significant differences as to how this procedure is conducted in each office. This chapter will study the laws and regulations, rules and procedures on appeals in two of the main patent offices in the world – the European Patent Office – EPO and the United States Patent and Trademark Office – USPTO, and in the Brazilian Patent Office – INPI, pointing out the main differences between them.

Keywords: appeal, patent, patent examination, industrial property, patent offices

1. Introduction

The right to appeal, in general, exists in several legal systems around the world responding to the two main characteristics of every human being. The first refers to the attitude of not settling for adverse decisions, which leads people to seek instruments to remediate these decisions, while the second is the possibility that every human being has to make mistakes and the need to correct these mistakes in decision-making acts that may have been mistaken [1].

Thus, an appeal is an instrument allowing for review of a decision made by a hierarchically higher instance aiming at its change or reversal. Appeals serve both as a process for correcting defective acts and as a process to find the actual and proper interpretation to a certain law or rule.

In the patent systems, appeals are primarily used to change or reverse an adverse decision by a first-instance patent examiner upon examination of the patentability of an application. This examination verifies compliance by the application with the legal provisions to become a patent. Among these provisions, attention is called to patentability requirements – novelty, inventive step, and industrial applicability – and patentability conditions – sufficiency of disclosure, clarity and/or support for the claims. When the patent examiner understands that any of these legal requirements and/or conditions is not met, the patent application is rejected.

Upon rejection of a patent application, a period for appeal against this decision begins. In the appeal procedure, a board of appeal or appeal division reviews the decision, taking the reasons that supported the first-instance administrative decision and the arguments of the parties into account, as to achieve a more proper decision for such case.

All patent offices have procedures for appeal against first instance administrative decisions taken by these offices, which are governed by specific laws, rules, and procedures. This chapter will study how appeals work in two of the main patent offices in the world, the European Patent Office – EPO and the United States Patent and Trademark Office – USPTO and in the Brazilian Patent Office – INPI, pointing out the main differences between them.

2. European patent office

The first relevant point of appeal procedure in the European patent system is that, unlike in the USPTO and INPI, appeals are not administrative proceedings. Although they exist in the EPO organizational structure, they are legal procedures under the responsibility of the boards of appeal [2, 3].

Boards of appeals are the second and final instances of the EPO, being independent of such office and only governed by the European Patent Convention (EPC). They are divided into four boards: enlarged board of appeal; legal board of appeal; technical boards of appeal; and disciplinary board of appeal.

Any party to the first-instance proceedings that led to the contested decision and that have been adversely affected by a decision of the receiving section, examining divisions, opposition divisions, and the legal division of the EPO may appeal to the Boards of Appeal.[1] In this regard, appeals may be divided into *ex parte* procedures, i.e., there is only one party to the appeal procedures, and *inter partes*, i.e., there are two or more parties to the appeal procedures. *Inter partes* appeal procedures occur when appealed decisions are taken by the opposition divisions, while *ex parte* procedures occur when the decisions are taken by the examining division. When there is more than one party to the appeal, the party filing the appeal is called the appellant, while the other parties are "parties of right" [2–4].

Although decisions taken by any of the EPO departments already mentioned can be appealed, technical decisions related to the patentability of a patent application or a patent already granted are those taken by the examining and opposition divisions. Examples of these types of decisions are those rejecting a patent application, in case of examining divisions, or decisions to revoke a patent or reject an opposition, in case of opposition divisions. It is worth noting that the European patent

1 Articles 106 and 107, EPC.

system, unlike Brazil, allows for filing an appeal against the granting of a patent in cases in which the grant was based on a text not previously approved by the applicant [4].

Appeals in the European patent system have suspensive and devolutive effects. The suspensive effect suspends the effects of the appealed decision until a decision on the appeal is rendered by the boards of appeal. For example, if the opposition division decides to cancel a patent and the patentee files an appeal, the patent shall continue having its effects until the boards of appeal take a decision. On its turn, the devolutive effect, except for the interlocutory revision procedure to be addressed below, transfers the power to decide such case from the first-instance examining division to the boards of appeal [3].

Three actions are required to begin the appeal procedure: (a) filing of a notice of appeal within two months of notification of the appealed decision; (b) payment of an appeal fee, within the same period; and (c) within four months of notification of the decision, a statement setting out the grounds of appeal shall be filed.[2] If the appellant fails to file the notice of appeal or to pay the fee within the established period, the appeal is deemed not filed [2, 4].

Once the appeal is filed, in case of *ex parte* procedures, it is forwarded to the division responsible for assessing the possibility of an interlocutory revision.[3] This procedure consists in an evaluation of the appeal by the examining division responsible for the appealed decision itself. If this division considers the appeal to be admissible and well-founded, it may rectify its decision or, if new objections are raised and not previously discussed, proceed with the examination. Three reasons, for example, may explain a change in a decision under appeal by the own first-instance division responsible for the decision: (a) the division made a mistake by not considering a certain part of the material available; (b) the division did not receive the material filed within the EPO on time due to an error by the EPO itself, or; (c) the division's decision is not incorrect, but the presentation of new evidence, facts, or changes in the application overcomes the objections that led to the appealed decision [5].

Nonetheless, if the appeal is not examined or allowed by the examining division within three months of receipt of the statement of the grounds of appeal, it shall be remitted to the Board of Appeal without delay, and without comment as to its merit. As it only applies to *ex parte* procedures, this mechanism is not valid for decisions by the opposition divisions that, as already mentioned, always have at least two parties, the opponent and the patentee. If the appeal is received by the boards of appeal, the examining division cannot interfere thereon anymore. The mechanism of interlocutory revision is very useful to prevent cases that can be easily reversed from getting to the boards of appeal, saving quite some time.

Upon filing of the appeal, it will be examined for admissibility and, among other factors, the following points will be assessed: (a) if the decision is appealable, (b) if the appellant has the right to appeal, (c) if the deadlines were respected, (d) if the fee was paid, (e) if the notice of appeal and the statement of grounds meet the requirements in Rule 99 of the EPC [2, 4].

The statement of grounds of appeal shall contain a party's complete appeal case. Accordingly, it shall set out clearly and concisely the reasons why it is requested that the decision under appeal be reversed, and should specify expressly all the facts,

[2] Article 108 of the EPC.

[3] Article 109 of the EPC.

arguments and evidence relied on.[4] Pursuant to rule 12 [4] of the rules of procedure of the boards of appeal (RPBOA), these boards may use their discretion when admitting new submissions in the appeal procedure, i.e., when admitting facts, evidence, and/or objections not submitted during the first-instance procedure. Nonetheless, such submissions should be made preferably at the beginning of the appeal procedure, and the acceptance thereof by the board of appeals during the second-instance proceeding is at the board's discretion. In this sense, these boards have been adopting a restrictive stance in accepting late submissions. In order to accept or not late submissions to the appeal procedure, the boards consider, among others, the following factors: the stage of processing of the appeal or whether the submission is detrimental to procedural economy and the complexity of the case[5] [6].

Some other principles not expressly defined in the EPC or the RPBOA, but that were established by decisions of the enlarged board of appeal, have been governing the appeal procedure in Europe. One of these principles establishes an important distinction between decisions by examining divisions and those by opposition divisions. When appeals come from opposition divisions, the boards of appeal cannot examine reasons that were not presented by the opponent during the first-instance proceeding and/or were not discussed by the opposition divisions, unless expressly authorized by the patentee. Nonetheless, the same restriction does not apply if the opposed decision is taken by the examining divisions, as in the case of an application rejection decision. In these cases, appeals are not restricted to the reasons that led to rejection of the patent application, and the boards of appeal may broaden their examination to patentability requirements or conditions that were not discussed at first instance.

During the appeal phase in the EPO, oral proceedings may occur at the request of the EPO itself or at the request of any other party to the appeal. When oral proceedings occur during the appeal, they are public, unlike those occurring before the examining divisions.[6] In cases of oral proceedings, the Board of Appeal may provide a preliminary opinion on the matter within four months of this proceeding, enabling the appellant to assess its chances of success in the appeal.[7]

Regarding the powers of the boards of appeal in deciding appeals, article 111 (1) of the EPC determines that the boards may either exercise any power within the competence of the first-instance department which was responsible for the decision appealed or remit the case to that department for further prosecution. At this point, article 11 of the RPBOA advices the board not to remit a case to the department whose decision was appealed for further prosecution, unless special reasons present themselves for doing so. As a rule, fundamental deficiencies which are apparent in the proceedings before that department constitute such special reasons [2, 6]. The decisions of the boards of appeal are unappealable. Nonetheless, as an exception, it is possible, under certain conditions, to request review by the enlarged board of appeal.[8]

Figure 1 shows a schematic presentation of the procedures for appeal against rejections in the EPO.

---

4 Article 99 (2) of the EPC and Article 12 (3) of the RPBOA.

5 Article 13 of the RPBOA.

6 Article 116 of the EPC.

7 Article 15 of the RPBOA.

8 Article 112a of the EPC.

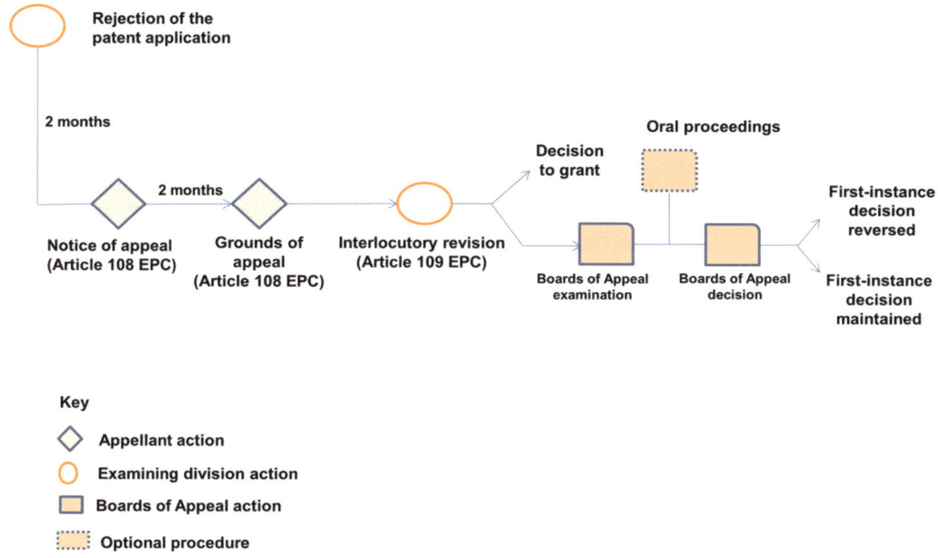

Figure 1.
Schematic representation of the procedure for appeal against rejection in the EPO.

3. United States patent and trademark office

An important difference of the United States patent system compared to the Brazilian system, for example, is the fact that several are the possible paths in the USPTO after a second or subsequent rejection of some claims in a patent application. The applicant may file a request for continued examination (RCE),[9] file for an amendment after final (AAF),[10] abandon the application, apply for a continuation-in-part,[11] or file a request for appeal [7, 8].

Appeals in the United States patent system aim to review objections related to the patentability of claims in a patent application and may be filed after a second action by the office rejecting some of these claims. These procedures, at the administrative level of the USPTO, are conducted by three administrative judges of the Patent Trial and Appeal Board (PTAB), which is the second-instance administrative body responsible for patents in this office. These judges must be people with technical and legal knowledge. The duties of this Board are: (a) to review decisions rejecting claims in patent applications; (b) to review reexamination appeals;[12] (c) to conduct derivation proceeding,[13]

[9] Request for Continued Examination (RCE). This is a request to reopen the processing of the patent application yet at first instance through the payment of a specific fee, where the examiner will evaluate the changes in the claims and the arguments presented [8].

[10] Amendment after final (AAF). It is the filing of amendments to claims. This procedure, unlike the RCE, is free of charge; however, the examiner has little time to examine it [8].

[11] Continuation-in-part. A request for continuation of an original patent application, where a new matter or new claims are included in the application. This procedure does not end the first-instance proceeding for the new matter included.

[12] Reexamination. Procedure that can be requested by anyone, at any time during the term of a patent, aiming at reviewing a patent already granted.

[13] Derivation proceeding. This is a trial proceeding conducted at the Board to determine whether (i) an inventor named in an earlier application derived the claimed invention from an inventor named in the petitioner's application, and (ii) the earlier application claiming such invention was filed without authorization.

(d) to conduct *inter partes* review;[14] and post-grant review.[15] Each of these procedures is conducted by a jury composed of at least three members of the board, who shall be appointed by the Director [9].

The USPTO's appeal procedure begins with the submission of a notice of appeal and payment of the required fee within no more than six months after the decision denying the patentability of the claims. Then, within a period of two months, which can be extended in exceptional situations for up to five months, the appeal brief must be filed with the office, including, in addition to the applicant's arguments regarding each of the objections raised by the examiner, other information, such as the name of the interested party, a concise explanation of the matter defined in each independent claim that has been rejected, and an appendix containing a copy of the claims under appeal [10].

A pilot program in progress at the USPTO provides the possibility of filing a pre-appeal request with the notice of appeal, where the applicant may request a review of the decision rejecting the claims. This request may not exceed five pages and must provide a series of succinct, concise, and focused arguments explaining the reasons why the review is being requested. This request is assessed by a panel of three examiners, including the examiner responsible for the decision to reject the claims. There are four possible outcomes for this review: (a) the request will continue under appeal, as the reasons were not sufficient; (b) the first-instance proceeding will be reopened; (c) the claims are accepted and, (d) the pre-appeal request does not meet the requirements and is disregarded [9].

After the appeal brief is filed with the USPTO, it does not immediately enter the jurisdiction of the appeal board. Appeals are first examined at an appeal conference, whose participants are the examiner responsible for the decision to reject the claims him/herself, his/her supervisor, and a third examiner who is able to consider the merits of the matter under appeal. After this procedure, the examiner may introduce new objections to reject the claims and reopen the case at first instance, may reverse the decision denying the claims, or may maintain the appeal, preparing a written response to the reasons for appeal. This reply must discuss all grounds for the challenged decision, enabling the examiner to add new objections to the request, if applicable.

After filing a notice of appeal with the USPTO, the filing of amendments to the application is not a matter of right. For acceptance of such amendments, two deadlines shall be considered and certain criteria shall be met. In the case these amendments are filed on the date or after the notice of appeal and before the appeal brief, such amendments may be accepted, as long as: (a) they cancel claims or comply with any requirement of form expressly set forth in a previous Office action; (b) they present rejected claims in better form for consideration, (c) they show good and sufficient reasons why the amendment is necessary and was not earlier presented.[16] Amendments filed on or after the date of filing a brief may not make substantive amendments to the claims, but may be admitted: (a) to cancel claims, where such cancelation does not affect the scope of any other pending claim in the proceeding, or (b) to rewrite dependent claims into independent form.[17] Amendments to the application are not accepted after the appeal enters the jurisdiction of the PTAB [10].

Like the filing of amendments to the application, the filing of new evidence or testimonies for inclusion in the application follows certain rules. If these amendments are

[14] Inter partes review. It is a trial proceeding conducted at the Board to review the patentability of one or more claims in a patent based on novelty and inventive step and only on the basis of prior art consisting of patents or printed publications.

[15] Post-grant review. It is a trial proceeding conducted at the Board to review the patentability of one or more claims on any ground and any matter of the prior art.

[16] 37 CFR § 1.116.

[17] 37 CFR § 41.33.

filed at the time of or after filing the notice of appeal, but before the appeal brief, these amendments may be accepted if the examiner understands that: (a) such evidence and/or testimonies surpass all objections under appeal; (b) show good and sufficient reasons as to why the amendment is necessary and was not previously filed. In all other cases, they shall be rejected. New evidence may not be filed together with the brief.

In case a new objection to the application is added to the examiner's written response to the appeal brief, the appellant has two options: apply for a reopening of the proceeding at first instance or request that the appeal is maintained by filing, within two months, a reply to the examiner's opinion. Only after expiration of the deadline to file the reply with the office, the appeal is forwarded to the PTAB. In this reply, no amendments to the claims or new evidence are admitted.

In the American patent system, the appellant may request oral proceedings in circumstances in which the appellant thinks it is necessary or desirable for proper understanding of the appeal. This request is made in writing and shall be accompanied by the payment of a fee, within two months of the date of the examiner's response to the appeal brief, or on the date of filing of his/her reply.

After submission of the reply to the examiner's opinion, with or without oral proceedings, the three PTAB judges shall render the final decision, issuing a written decision, whose outcomes may be: (a) affirmance, a situation in which the examiner's decision of rejecting the claims is fully confirmed; (b) affirmance-in-part, a situation in which the examiner's decision of rejecting at least one of the claims is confirmed, but not all; (c) reversed, when the decision of denying the claims is not confirmed, and (d) new grounds for rejection, a situation in which the PTAB judges understand there are additional reasons for which at least one of the claims is not patentable. In this last case, the appellant has two options: apply for reopening of the proceeding at first instance and file amendments or evidence deemed necessary, or request a review of the case. In the review, the appellant shall define specifically where he or she believes the appeal board was mistaken.

Figure 2 shows a schematic presentation of the procedures for appeal against rejection in the USPTO.

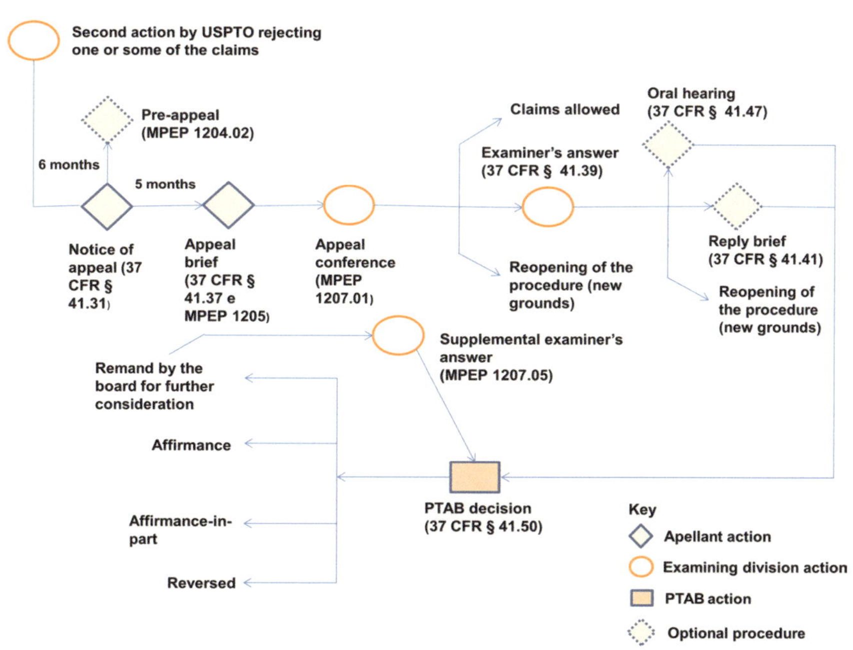

Figure 2.
Schematic representation of the procedure for appeal against rejection in the USPTO.

4. Brazilian patent office

In the Brazilian patent system, the instrument for administrative appeals is provided for in chapter 1 of title VII of Law No. 9,279 of 1996, the Brazilian IP Law (LPI). This chapter of the aforementioned Law addresses the applicable appeals against decisions rendered by INPI, therefore including decisions related to patent applications [11].

Appeals are filed voluntarily by anyone feeling aggrieved in their rights by a decision determining rejection of a patent application, aiming at changing such decision. This filing is made in up to sixty days after the decision rejecting the application is published in the Industrial Property Gazette (RPI),[18] through a written petition, observing the administrative principles of publicity and formalism [12].

Paragraph 2 of Article 212 of the LPI makes two important reservations about situations in which it is not possible to appeal against the INPI decisions regarding a patent application. The reservations are as follows: a decision determining the final dismissal of a patent application and a decision accepting the patent application. Therefore, it is clear, regarding the decisions on patentability of a patent application, that only decisions determining rejection of a patent application are subject to appeal [11].

Administrative appeals in the Brazilian patent system have suspensive and full devolutive effects, applying all provisions pertinent to examination in the first instance, in so far as they are applicable. The suspensive effect interrupts the effects of the contested act since the filing of the appeal until final decision, aiming to safeguard the right of the applicant and protect him against the damaging effects resulting from the appealed decision. The two major practical consequences of the suspensive effect are the interruption of the period of prescription[19] and the impossibility of filing a lawsuit against the act to be challenged while there is no decision on the appeal [13, 14].

On its turn, full devolutive effect means that the decided matter is fully referred to a higher hierarchical authority for acknowledgement and decision, which for INPI is represented by the President of the independent agency. This implies full review of the merits of the patent application under analysis by a second administrative instance coordination. In this case, as all relevant provisions applied in the examination at first instance are still valid, second-instance examiners may suggest amendments to the application, carry out new searches, and raise new objections to the application, even if these have not been discussed at first instance. Accordingly, the appellant is allowed, at second administrative instance, to come up with new evidence favoring the application patentability, and amend the specifications and its patent claim scope, as long as the same are limited to what was initially disclosed.

In the Brazilian patent system, third parties may be a party to administrative appeals under patent applications. The period therefor is sixty days, and the counter-arguments petition shall be filed under the appeal[20] [11, 12].

[18] The Industrial Property Gazette (RPI) communicates all INPI decisions to the general public by means of decision codes.

[19] The 5-year period for filing legal actions is interrupted.

[20] Article 213, LPI. Interested parties shall be summoned to file, within sixty (60) days, counter-arguments under the appeal.

Although decisions on appeals are the responsibility of the President of INPI, as these decisions involve technical matters related to many technologies, the substantive examination is actually performed by a specific coordination office reporting directly to the INPI Presidency – the General Coordination Office for Administrative Invalidation Proceedings and Appeals (CGREC). This coordination office is responsible, therefore, for the administrative processing of patent applications at second administrative instance, for matters related to industrial property.

The two main duties of CGREC are: the issuance of expert opinions in intellectual property matters to support the President of INPI, which is the authority competent by law to register them, and the search to consolidate an administrative case law on the matter[21] [15].

CGREC is currently divided into three technical coordination offices and one administrative support division. The CGREC division that deals with patents at second administrative instance is the Technical Coordination for Appeals and Administrative Invalidation Procedures for Patents (COREP), which is composed of eighteen patent examiners [16].

The following section shall present the administrative processing of patent applications at second instance in INPI.

4.1 Second-instance administrative proceedings for patent applications at INPI

Once a patent application has been rejected at first instance, the applicant may file an appeal, what must be done in up to sixty days, according to article 212 of the LPI. In case the applicant elects to file the appeal, a new procedural phase begins in INPI, which initiates with the admissibility exam; having the application satisfied the formal requirements,[22] decision code 12.2 is published in the Industrial Property Gazette.[23]

After publication of the appeal against rejection in the RPI, any interested party may file counter-arguments to the appeal, which are, in general, filed by third parties interested in the patent application, aiming at preservation of the rejection decision on the application. As appeals are fully referred to a higher instance, the second administrative instance completely reexamines the matter of the patent

[21] Article 15, DECREE No. 8,854/2016 – The General Coordination Office for Administrative Invalidation Proceedings and Appeals is responsible for: I – examining and providing technical support for the decisions of the President of INPI in administrative invalidation proceedings and appeals filed pursuant to the prevailing industrial property laws and regulations, and issuing opinions on the matter raised; II – examining and providing technical support for the decisions of the President of INPI in the appeals regarding intellectual property, which registration is under the responsibility of INPI by law; III – guiding and coordinating the systematization, organization, and update of administrative decisions related to intellectual and industrial property, seeking to consolidate an administrative case law on matter; and IV – proposing improvements to the guidelines and procedures for examination of appeals and administrative invalidation proceedings filed pursuant to prevailing intellectual and industrial property laws and regulations.

[22] In the admissibility examination, it is verified whether the appeal is applicable, if it is timely, and if the fee was paid.

[23] Decision code 12.2 indicates that an appeal was filed aiming at a new examination of the matter by the president of INPI.

application, applying all relevant legal provisions employed in the first-instance examination.

In the examination of the patent application by the second instance, the examiner uses all documentation filed at the first instance (expert opinions, petitions, amendments to the application, supporting information, etc.), as well as any new information filed by the appellant in with the appeal petition or by interested parties in the counter-arguments petition, if any. After the first second-instance examination, there are four possible outcomes for the patent application: the appeal is granted (decision code 100), the appeal is denied (decision code 111), non-patentability opinion (decision code 120) or technical requirements (decision code 121). In the decision to grant the appeal, the second-instance examiner understands that the application meets the legal requirements and conditions, draws up an opinion pointing out the parts of the documentation that shall compose the patent, and refers the application for decision of the President of INPI. In the decision to make requirements, like in the first instance, the second-instance examiner understands that the application or part of it has patentability conditions; however, it shows irregularities that prevent patenting as it is. For this reason, they issue an opinion requesting the appellant to meet certain requirements in order for the application to meet patentability requirements and conditions. When the examiner understands that the application does not meet the patentability requirements and/or conditions, he/she may decide to deny the appeal, a situation in which it is no longer possible to discuss it, and the application is forwarded to the President for decision, or he/she may issue a non-patentability opinion, situation in which new arguments and/or documents of the state-of-the-art are presented by the examiner or further clarifications by the applicant may be necessary.

During examination, the second-instance examiner evaluates the same legal requirements and conditions as the first-instance examiner and uses the same Normative Instructions and Examination Guidelines. **Figures 3–5** show a schematic representation of the procedural flow of patent applications at second instance in INPI.

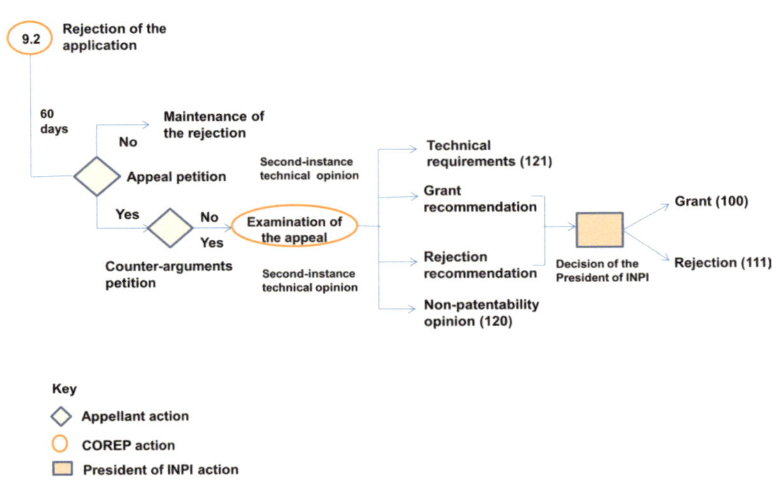

Figure 3.
Schematic representation of the procedural flow of patent applications at second administrative instance in INPI.

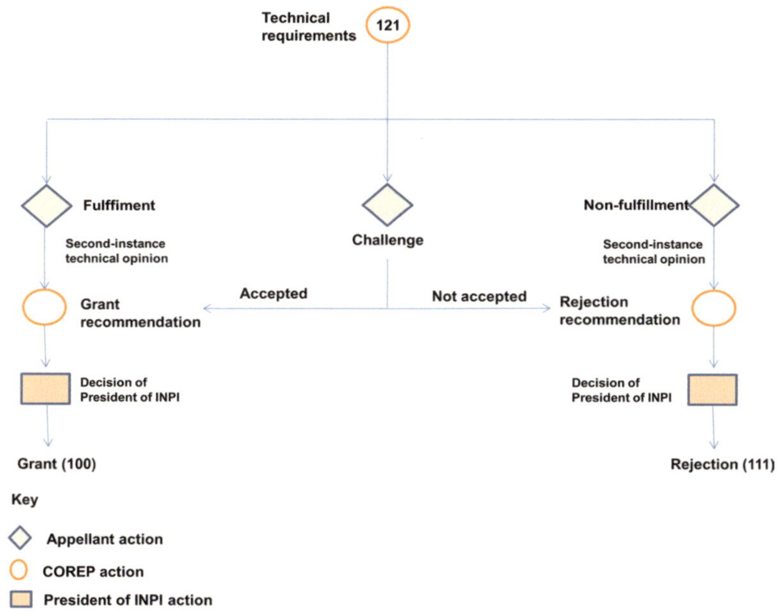

Figure 4.
Schematic representation of the procedural flow of patent applications after technical requirements in INPI.

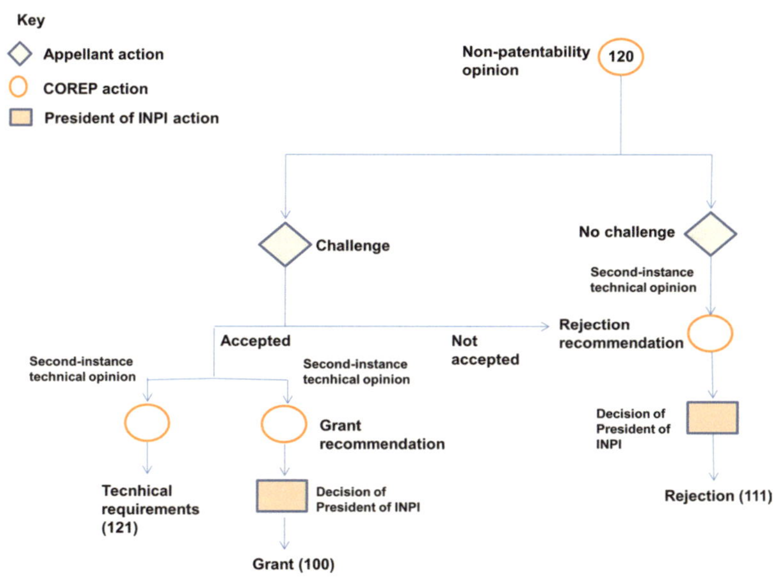

Figure 5.
Schematic representation of the procedural flow of patent applications after technical requirements in INPI.

5. Final considerations

As it was evidenced, although the three patent offices have procedures for appeal against first-instance decisions, there are significant differences in the procedures of each of these offices, starting with the type of proceeding. While in the EPO it is a legal proceeding, in the USPTO and in INPI, it is an administrative proceeding. There are also differences in the types of appealable decisions in each office.

Regarding decisions related to the examination of the application patentability, in Brazil only decisions rejecting patent applications are subject to appeal. In Europe, in addition to decisions rejecting patent applications, the decisions by opposition divisions are also subject to appeal, in other words, those determining rejection of the opposition and maintenance of a patent in its full or amended form or those setting out the cancelation of the patent.

In the specific case of procedures for appeal against decisions rejecting a patent application, these offices also differ regarding the terms, the rules for filing new submissions, the existence of a review mechanism before analysis by the board of appeals, as well as the participation by interested third parties.

Regarding deadlines, the EPO and the USPTO present different deadlines for filing the notice of appeal and the grounds of the appeal. At INPI, both the notice of appeal and its grounds shall be filed together, within a maximum period of two months of the notice of the decision to reject the patent application.

All offices, as long as pursuant to certain conditions, permit amendments to the claims and/or filing of new evidence after the notice of appeal. In the case of the EPO, these submissions shall be filed preferably at the beginning of the appeal procedure, and the boards may accept or not, at their discretion, new submissions during the appeal procedure. In the USPTO, the filing of new evidence and/or amendments to the claims is also subject to certain rules; however, it is important to highlight that these submissions shall be filed before the appeal is sent to the PTAB, and no new submission shall be accepted after that date. In INPI, the filing of new evidence and/or amendments to the claims is accepted throughout the processing of the appeal. However, the filing of amendments to the claims is subject to the provisions in Article 32 of the LPI.[24]

Unlike INPI, both the USPTO and the EPO have a mechanism for the first-instance department responsible for the decision to review its own appealed decisions before they are forwarded to the boards of appeal. This mechanism allows for quick resolution of some cases, with significant economy of time and resources.

INPI, unlike the EPO and the USPTO, has a mechanism for participation of interested third parties in the procedure for appeal against the rejection, the so-called counter-arguments to the appeal, which allows any interested parties to submit the reasons why they understand that the decision of rejecting a patent application shall be upheld. Regarding the effects of the appeal, both in Europe as in Brazil, the suspensive and devolutive effects apply.

Table 1 briefly presents the main differences in the appeal procedures of the three offices analyzed.

Results obtained through a comparative study enabled to identify good practices related to appeals adopted in two of the main patent offices in the world with potential for application in INPI. Among these practices, it is important to note the existence of a mechanism for reviewing the challenged decision by the first-instance department responsible for such decision, like the interlocutory revision mechanism adopted in the EPO, for example. Implementation of a mechanism similar to that in INPI is currently under evaluation by the Institute. If implemented, INPI may greatly improve its efficiency, considering that decisions that may be easily reversed, whether because of new evidence submitted or because of submission of new patent claim scopes overcoming the objections made in the first instance, may be reversed in a more speedy and economic way, with no need

[24] Article 32 of the LPI provides that amendments to the claims are not accepted when they add information to what was initially provided or broaden the scope of protection of the claims in comparison with the claims filed until the request for examination of the patent application.

	EPO	USPTO	INPI
Type of proceeding	Legal	Administrative	Administrative
Appealable decisions (regarding patentability)	Rejection Maintenance of a patent Revocation of a patent	Second or subsequent decision rejecting one or more claims	Rejection
Filing of appeal	2 months	Up to 6 months	2 months
Reason for appeal	4 months	Up to 11 months	2 months
New submissions[1]	YES	YES	YES
First-instance revision	YES	YES	NO
Counter-arguments[2]	NO	NO	YES
Effects	Suspensive Devolutive	—	Suspensive Full devolutive
Oral proceedings	YES	YES	NO

[1]*In all offices, the submission of new claims and/or evidence to the proceeding is subject to specific rules.*
[2]*The results presented in this row of the table refer specifically to appeals against a decision rejecting a patent application.*

Table 1.
Comparative table of the appeal procedures in the EPO, the USPTO, and INPI.

for evaluation by a new examiner or collegiate. It is worth noting that by shedding light on the laws, regulations, and procedures for appeals in three important patent offices, highlighting the practices adopted in each office, this study may contribute for the applicant to increase his/her chances of success in the appeal stage in these three patent offices studied.

Author details

Fabio Monteiro dos Santos[1]*, Heleno José Costa Bezerra Netto[2] and Ricardo Carvalho Rodrigues[1]

1 Brazilian National Institute of Industrial Property (Intellectual Property Academy), Rio de Janeiro, Brazil

2 Brazilian National Institute of Industrial Property (General Coordination Office for Administrative Invalidation Proceedings and Appeals—CGREC), Rio de Janeiro, Brazil

*Address all correspondence to: fabios@inpi.gov.br

IntechOpen

© 2021 The Author(s). Licensee IntechOpen. This chapter is distributed under the terms of the Creative Commons Attribution License (http://creativecommons.org/licenses/by/3.0), which permits unrestricted use, distribution, and reproduction in any medium, provided the original work is properly cited. CC BY

References

[1] Dalla Pace, C. A sistematização dos recursos administrativos na legislação federal. Dissertação. São Paulo: Faculdade de Direito, Universidade de São Paulo; 2015.

[2] European Patent Convention (EPC). 16th edition; 2016.

[3] European Patent Office (EPO). Case Law of the Boards of Appeal [Internet]; 2019. Available at: https://www.epo.org/law-practice/case-law-appeals/case-law.html. [Retrieved on: 2021-09-03]

[4] Veronese, A. Appeal procedure before the European Patent Office. In: Toshiko Takenaka, editor. Patent Law and Theory. A Handbook of Contemporary Research. Cheltenham: Edward Elgar Publishing Limited; 2008. P. 224-245.

[5] European Patent Office (EPO). Guidelines for the Examination in the European Patent Office; 2019.

[6] European Patent Office (EPO). Rules of procedure of the Boards of Appeal; 2020.

[7] Merril, S.A, Elliot, G.C.A. A patent primer. In: A Patent System for the 21st Century. Washington, D.C: The National Academies Press, 2004. (COMPLETAR REFERÊNCIA)

[8] Yospin, M.M. Final rejection: not the end. Yospin Law [Internet]. 2019. Available at: https://www.yospinlaw.com/2019/08/12/final-rejection [Retrieved on: 2020-05-22].

[9] United States Patent and Trademark Office (USPTO). Manual of Patent Examining Procedure [Internet]. 2014. Available at: https://www.uspto.gov/web/offices/pac/mpep/index.html [Retrieved on: 2021-03-09].

[10] Code of Federal Regulations. Title 37. Patents, Trademarks and Copyrights [Internet]. 2019. Available at: https://www.govinfo.gov/content/pkg/CFR-2019-title37-vol1/html/CFR-2019-title37-vol1.htm [Retrieved on: 2021-03-09].

[11] Brasil. Law No. 9,279 of May 14, 1996. Provides for industrial property rights and obligations. Diário Oficial da República Federativa do Brasil. [Internet]. 1996. Available at: http://www.planalto.gov.br/ccivil_03/leis/l9279.htm [Retrieved on: 2021-03-09]

[12] Brasil. Law No. 9,784 of January 29, 1999. Provides for administrative proceedings at the Federal Administration level. [Internet] Available at: http://www.planalto.gov.br/ccivil_03/leis/l9784.htm [Retrieved on: 2020-05-23]

[13] IDS-Instituto Dannemann Siemsen de Estudos Jurídicos e Técnicos. Comentários à lei da propriedade industrial. Edição revista e atualizada. Rio de Janeiro: Renovar. 2005. 548p.

[14] Meirelles, H.L., Filho, J.E.B., Burle, C.R. Direito administrativo brasileiro. 42ª ed. São Paulo: Malheiros, 2016. 975p.

[15] Brasil. Decree No. 8,854 of September 22, 2016. [Internet] Available at: http://www.planalto.gov.br/ccivil_03/_Ato2015-2018/2016/Decreto/D8854.htm. [Retrieved on: 2021-03-09]

[16] Instituto Nacional da Propriedade Industrial (INPI). Portaria nº 210, de 1º de julho de 2015.